The Early Childhood Career Lattice
Perspectives on Professional Development

The Early Childhood Career Lattice
Perspectives on Professional Development

Julienne Johnson and Janet B. McCracken, Editors

National Association for the Education of Young Children

National Institute for Early Childhood Professional Development

Washington, D.C.

A 1993–94 NAEYC Comprehensive Membership benefit

Photographs—p. 1, 5, 25, 36, 43, 47, 73, 96, 154—Subjects & Predicates; p. 2, 32, 64—Nancy P. Alexander; p. 12, 104, 107, 161, 180—Robert Hill; p. 60—Rick Reinhard; p. 66—Shelby M. Forrest; p. 80—Toni H. Liebman; p. 101—BmPorter/Don Franklin; p. 122—J.D. Images; p. 170—Loren Fogelman.

National Association for the Education of Young Children (NAEYC)
1509 16th Street, N.W.
Washington, DC 20036-1426
202-232-8777   800-424-2460

ISBN: 0-935989-60-9
NAEYC #792

Design/production—Melanie Rose White

Printed in the United States of America

Acknowledgment

NAEYC gratefully acknowledges the Carnegie Corporation of New York for their support of the National Institute for Early Childhood Professional Development, and especially Michael Levine, Program Officer, for his leadership and support of initiatives designed to improve the quality of services for young children and enhance early childhood professional development.

Contents

Introduction

Sue Bredekamp and Barbara Willer

NAEYC's mission is to improve the quality of services available for young children from birth through age 8 and their families. In working toward this goal for a growing and diverse field, NAEYC provides professional development opportunities; sets and promotes standards for high-quality programs and professional preparation; and develops and disseminates publications and materials that address developmentally appropriate early childhood education.

NAEYC has strived to improve professional preparation and practice since its founding in 1926. The Association's long-standing tradition of support for professional development is evident in its instrumental role in national initiatives including Head Start, the Child Development Associate (CDA) national credentialing program, and most recently the National Academy of Early Childhood Programs.

Although during the last decade debates in the field about the goals of early childhood professionalism were marked by a lack of consensus, several initiatives were launched toward the goal of improving the professional development and status of early childhood educators. Efforts to achieve professionalism took several directions. The Center for Career Development in Early Care and Education began operation at Wheelock College in 1990. Its purpose is to address planning and policy issues about career development for all types of early childhood programs. The Child Care Employee Project (renamed the National Center for the Early Childhood Work Force in 1993), in collaboration with many organizations including NAEYC, started another professional development strategy in 1991—the Worthy Wage campaign—to raise the awareness of the public and practitioners about the integral connection between compensation of staff and quality of care for children.

In 1991, NAEYC further formalized its quest for professionalism when it launched the National Institute for Early Childhood Professional Development. Made possible by a start-up grant from Carnegie Corporation of New York, the Institute is designed to enhance the quality of care and education for young children by improving the quality and consistency of early childhood professional preparation and development.

A vision for a systems approach to early childhood professional development was first proposed by the Institute in *Young Children* (Bredekamp, 1991). The Institute's dream is for all programs for young children—child care centers, family child care homes, preschools, kindergartens, primary schools—to provide high-quality, developmentally appropriate early childhood education. This vision of professional development has several dimensions:

The Institute is designed to enhance the quality and consistency of early childhood professional development.

The lattice connotes upward mobility with enhanced qualifications and improved compensation, while conveying horizontal movement across the various sectors of the diverse field.

- A coordinated, articulated career development system will be available and accessible to individuals who choose to work with young children in a variety of settings.

- The quality and consistency of professional preservice and in-service preparation programs will be improved so that participation in such programs is clearly linked to improvements in practice.

- A variety of paths will be open to individuals to improve their professional qualifications, resulting in more steps than walls.

- Compensation will be commensurate with responsibilities of the position and qualifications and competence of individuals.

- Bridges will exist between systems that license child care programs and systems that certify teachers in the same state, allowing for horizontal as well as vertical movement across systems of employment.

- The false but enduring dichotomy between care and education in both perceptions and policies will be eliminated.

To achieve this vision, the Institute conceptualized a complex professional development system with numerous strands bound together by a

Individuals in early childhood education must build and maintain consensus regarding the best practices for serving children and families.

shared core of knowledge—symbolized by a career lattice (Bredekamp & Willer, 1992). This lattice connotes upward mobility with enhanced qualifications and improved compensation, while conveying horizontal movement across the various sectors of the diverse field. A conceptual framework for this professional development system developed by Barbara Willer and Sue Bredekamp was adopted by NAEYC's Governing Board in November 1993 and appears in its entirety immediately following this introduction (NAEYC, 1994).

In a related effort to recognize—and then to challenge, resolve, and move beyond—the barriers to the quest for professionalism in early childhood, the Institute brings the field's leaders together in annual conferences. This volume, compiled from presentations at the 1992 and 1993 events, reiterates the recurring questions; identifies components of the core knowledge of the profession; shares some promising practices and models for professional development; and offers insights into pursuit of the vision of a coordinated, articulated profession.

The official position of NAEYC appears as the conceptual framework. The other articles in this volume are the opinions (sometimes strong opinions) of the authors.

The goal of creating a dynamic, high-quality professional development system requires that individuals in early childhood education build and maintain consensus regarding the best practices for serving children and families, and then assure that these practices form the basis for professional preparation. Possibilities for reaching consensus, and unifying the system, are extended throughout these pages.

References

Bredekamp, S. (1991). A vision for early childhood professional development. *Young Children, 47*(1), 35–37.

Bredekamp, S., & Willer, B. (1992). Of ladders and lattices, cores and cones: Conceptualizing an early childhood professional development system. *Young Children, 47*(3), 47–50.

National Association for the Education of Young Children. (1994). NAEYC position statement: A conceptual framework for early childhood professional development. *Young Children, 49*(3), 68–77.

A Conceptual Framework for Early Childhood Professional Development

NAEYC Position Statement, Adopted November 1993

Edited by Barbara Willer

Introduction

For more than 60 years, the National Association for the Education of Young Children (NAEYC) has worked to promote high-quality early childhood programs for all young children and their families. Two major strands of activity support this goal: (1) facilitating the professional development of individuals working for and with young children from birth through age 8, and (2) improving public understanding and support for high-quality early childhood programs.

NAEYC's efforts have helped to create growing recognition of the importance of high-quality early childhood programs to our society and an increasing demand for services. Nonetheless, serious barriers remain that undermine access to high-quality services for all young children. There is increasing recognition that systemic approaches are required to address these barriers. A growing number of states and communities are employing comprehensive planning efforts to improve their early childhood care and education systems. Although these efforts vary considerably by state and community, there is typically recognition of the following key elements (NASBE, 1991; Melaville, Blank, & Asayesh, 1993; Morgan et al., 1993; Galinsky, Shubilla, Willer, Levine, & Daniel, 1994; Kagan & the *Quality 2000* Essentials Task Force, 1994):

1. a holistic approach to the needs of children and their families that stresses collaborative planning and service integration across traditional boundaries of child care, education, health, and social services;

2. systems that promote and recognize quality through licensing, regulation, and accreditation;

3. an effective system of early childhood professional development that provides meaningful opportunities for career advancement to ensure a well-qualified and stable work force;

4. equitable financing that ensures access for all children and families to high-quality services; and

5. active involvement of all players—providers, practitioners, parents, and community leaders from both public and private sectors—in all aspects of program planning and delivery.

NAEYC, working in conjunction with many other groups, is addressing each of these issues. NAEYC's leadership has been especially important in defining quality standards for programs for young children and for early childhood professional preparation programs. NAEYC standards for programs for children include its accreditation system and standards for high quality in early childhood programs, developmentally appropriate practice, and appropriate curriculum and assessment. NAEYC's National Institute for Early Childhood Professional Development fosters the development of a comprehensive, articulated system of professional development for **all** individuals working in **all** early childhood settings, recognizing that individuals will pursue different career paths and will bring different experiences, resources, and needs to the preparation process.

NAEYC believes that efforts to promote a high-quality system for early childhood professional development can be a catalyst to successfully address barriers to high quality for all young children and their families. As greater consensus is gained regarding the specialized skills and knowledge needed for effective early childhood practice, there will be greater expectations and demands for such knowledge and practice, requiring a corresponding increase in support for adequate financing of program resources—including staff compensation commensurate with qualifications and responsibilities.

Accordingly, NAEYC has developed the following conceptual framework that identifies key principles of an effective professional development system embedded within the larger system of effective early childhood service delivery. The framework includes several components. It begins with a statement of need that describes the current diversity of early childhood service providers and preparation opportunities and outlines the assumptions upon which this framework is built. The second component uses the analogy of a "lattice" to describe the professional knowledge, performances, and dispositions connected with the early childhood profession's diverse roles, levels, and settings. The third component describes key elements regarding the provision of professional

Efforts to promote a high-quality system for early childhood professional development can be a catalyst to successfully address barriers to high quality for all young children and their families.

development opportunities. The fourth and final component describes guidelines for compensation that link increases in professional development and improved performance to increased compensation.

This framework is intended to guide decision making related to early childhood professional development. It may be used by individuals making decisions regarding their own professional development, by early childhood programs making personnel decisions and policies and designing in-service training, by institutions of higher education and other community-based programs involved in the provision of early childhood professional development opportunities, and by policymakers and others concerned with the provision of early childhood services. The framework does not attempt to impose a prescriptive model, rather it identifies key principles and premises that apply across the diverse roles and settings of the early childhood profession.

The need for a unifying framework

NAEYC defines *early childhood education* to include any part- or full-day group program in a center, school, or home that serves children from birth through age 8, including children with special developmental and learning needs. This definition includes programs in child care centers, both for-profit and nonprofit; private and public prekindergarten programs; Head Start programs; family child care; and kindergartens, primary grades, and before- and after-school programs in elementary schools. These programs are operated under a variety of auspices and rely upon different funding systems, different regulatory structures, and different mechanisms to prepare and certify individuals to work with young children from birth through age 8, as briefly described in the following paragraphs.

The diversity of early childhood service providers

The diversity of services within the early childhood field reflects its roots in both social welfare and education. Although there has always been considerable overlap between these two traditions, especially among professionals, public perceptions presume distinct differences. "Child care" has traditionally been assumed to mean providing care for children whose parents are unavailable to provide full-time care because of a job or other circumstances. Child care centers and family child care homes typically offer a full-day schedule to correspond to parents' work hours and are typically regulated by state departments of human services through facility licensure (or registration in the case of family child care homes). Staff preparation and qualification requirements are sometimes included in these regulations, although they are minimal even when they exist. As a result, many individuals working in centers and family child care homes enter the field without previous professional preparation, but they gain professional knowledge and skills on the job.

Early childhood education is also rooted in the tradition of part-day preschool and nursery programs, traditionally assumed to promote children's social and educational development without consideration of parental needs for full-day programs. Part-day preschool programs operated within the private sector are subject to child care facility licensure in approximately half of the states. In some states programs may follow regulatory procedures for private schools. Professional qualifications for staff may or may not be included in these regulations.

The federally funded Head Start program has historically operated primarily as a part-day preschool program with comprehensive services, including health, nutrition, social services, and parent involvement. Head Start programs are required to meet federal performance standards and may also be required to meet state child care licensing regulations. Federal law requires that at least one teacher in a Head Start classroom possess a Child Development Associate (CDA) credential, its equivalent, or other early childhood degree as of 1994.

Prompted in part by the success of Head Start, more and more public education funds have been invested in preschool programs in recent years.

Prompted in part by the success of Head Start, more and more public education funds have been invested in preschool programs in recent years. These public school prekindergarten programs, now offered in the majority of states, are usually a part-day program. Like Head Start, these programs are typically targeted at children deemed at risk of later school failure, but unlike Head Start most are not designed as comprehensive child and family services. Personnel requirements in public prekindergarten programs typically exceed child care licensing requirements for specialized early childhood preparation but may or may not meet teacher licensure requirements for elementary and secondary education of at least a baccalaureate degree and may not require a specialized early childhood degree.

Early childhood education services also encompass services for young school-age children attending kindergarten through Grade 3, and before- and after-school programs. Kindergarten may be a part-day or full school-day program with teachers certified by the state, following teacher licensure requirements. Elementary grades, also operated on a typical school day that does not conform to most parents' work day, are taught by licensed teachers. Often, state teacher licensure (certification) requirements do not fully address the specialized skills, knowledge, and supervised practicum experience of work with younger children. Before- and after-school programs are increasingly needed because of the growing number of dual-earner or single-parent families. School-age child care programs are offered by schools and a variety of private agencies, as well as in family child care homes. Regardless of public or private sources of funding, qualifications for school-age child care personnel are more similar to those included in child care facility licensure than public school teacher licensure.

Increasing attention to serving children with disabilities has had considerable impact on the provision of early childhood services. The Individuals with Disabilities Education Act (IDEA) provides grants for states to provide interdisciplinary, family-based services for infants and toddlers with disabilities or developmental delays, as well as programs for similarly diagnosed preschool children. One of the basic principles of the IDEA is to provide services in the "least restrictive environment" or the most normalized setting appropriate for an individual child. This principle, along with the legal mandate established by the Americans with Disabilities Act (ADA) for public facilities—including child care centers and family child care homes—to make reasonable accommodations for individuals with disabilities, means that all early childhood personnel must be prepared to meet the needs of all children including those with special developmental and learning needs.

Diversity in early childhood professional preparation

Preparation programs are driven by the personnel requirements of the various service providers; personnel requirements are determined by their funding and regulatory structures. As a result, preparation programs for those working with young children are as disparate as the services themselves. Four- and five-year teacher education programs are driven by state teacher licensure (certification) requirements and often do not provide direct experience or preparation working with preschool children, especially infants and toddlers. When they do, they may focus more on theory and research than on practice and application. Programs in two-year institutions or community colleges typically stress working with younger children. Traditionally, two-year programs have taken one of two forms: technical programs in which transfer of credits is not the primary objective or programs designed to articulate with a baccalaureate program in which it is presumed that more professional course work will be taken at the upper levels. Some individuals begin their preparation in high-school vocational programs, sometimes articulated with community college programs and potentially baccalaureate degrees. This conceptual framework focuses primarily on postsecondary programs, presuming that individuals have obtained a high-school diploma or its equivalent. There is increasing recognition of the need to strengthen the school-to-work transition through vocational programs that more effectively prepare students entering the work world. Already some vocational programs are designed around the core early childhood competencies to provide supervised work experience in a variety of early childhood settings with children of various ages. As this trend continues, it will be important for the early childhood profession to recognize and incorporate this type of professional preparation as part of an overall system of professional development.

The challenges to be met

Despite the fact that *child care* and *early education* services are often funded and regulated by different agencies, the essential nature of the service varies little when done in an appropriate manner for an individual child. Although historical traditions have focused on *either* the child's needs for a program that promotes her or his development *or* meeting parents' need to provide child care when they are unavailable, there is increasing recognition that this represents a false dichotomy. Good programs must meet children's needs as well as families' needs. Moreover, it is increasingly clear that the teachers and caregivers who bring specialized knowledge and skills to their work are the best prepared to provide high-quality services to young children and their families.

There are significant barriers to improving early childhood professional development within each system. There is little incentive for individuals working in child care centers or family child care homes to seek specialized preparation for jobs that pay little more than minimum wage. In 1990 half of all teachers in child care centers nationally earned less than $11,000 annually, while the annual earnings of family child care providers *before expenses* averaged less than $10,000 per year (Willer, Hofferth, Kisker, Divine-Hawkins, Farquhar, & Glantz, 1991). It is unrealistic to expect those earning such wages to seek further professional preparation without additional reward. Those preparing to work in public schools may find that they are more attractive job candidates when they possess a more generalized teaching certificate (K–8) than specialized early childhood certification.

The increasing focus on full inclusion of children with disabilities in mainstreamed educational settings presents challenges both for early childhood special education professional preparation programs as well as those in general early childhood education. Traditional models that presumed separate classrooms with separate teaching staff are no longer acceptable and require the development of new models that build upon the strengths of the more specialized knowledge of early childhood special educators and the more generalist perspective of early childhood educators.

Assumptions

This conceptual framework bridges the historical divisions between child care and early education with a unifying and inclusive vision of high-quality services for all children and families and is based on the following assumptions:

- All young children, from birth through age 8, should have access to high-quality early childhood education services.
- Early childhood education is one part of a broad array of comprehensive services designed to foster individual children's optimal learning and development in all areas and to support families' child-rearing efforts, often necessitating early childhood professionals to work on interdisciplinary teams and to collaborate with a variety of service providers and agencies.
- Early childhood education programs occur in a variety of settings: centers, homes, and schools.
- The adults who work with young children and their families are key to providing high-quality programs.
- Parents and the public have every right to expect that adults employed in early childhood programs have the knowledge, dispositions, and skills needed to provide high-quality services.

This conceptual framework bridges the historical divisions between child care and early education with a unifying and inclusive vision of high-quality services for all children and families

- The early childhood profession is responsible for ensuring that its members meet and uphold high standards of professional practice.
- There are a variety of early childhood professional roles that require different types and levels of knowledge and skills but share a common core centered in early childhood education.
- Early childhood professionals include those working directly with young children and families as well as those working to support the provision of early childhood services to young children and their families.
- To attract and retain qualified adults to work in early childhood programs, there must be viable career options that provide opportunities for continued professional development and increased compensation.
- Early childhood professionals enter the field through various paths. Some individuals have completed professional preparation programs prior to assuming a professional role; for many others, formal professional preparation follows their decision to work with young children.
- Providing for a variety of early childhood professional roles with varying professional qualifications and responsibility (e.g., differentiated staffing patterns) allows individuals who have not yet acquired a recognized credential to work in early childhood program settings under the supervision of qualified professionals and provides increased recognition and remuneration to professionals who have achieved higher levels of expertise.
- Ongoing training and preparation opportunities should be structured to encourage and support all individuals working with young children to improve their professional knowledge and skills.
- Articulation mechanisms between various levels of preparation programs need to be strengthened.
- Mechanisms that transform diverse training and learning experiences into academic credit, such as assessment of experiential learning, must be readily accessible to early childhood practitioners.
- The early childhood profession must ensure that its members—in all roles and at all levels—reflect the ethnic and cultural diversity of our nation and its families.
- Barriers such as a lack of financial resources, as well as institutional racism and classism, that impede individuals from gaining and demonstrating the requisite knowledge for professional credentials must be challenged and removed.
- There must be greater public understanding of and support for the critical importance of the early years and also for the specialized skills and knowledge needed to work effectively with young children and their families.
- A greater investment of financial resources—both public and private— is needed to support the provision of high-quality early childhood services for all young children and their families.

A conceptual framework of early childhood professional development must achieve a balance between inclusivity and exclusivity. It must fully embrace the diversity of roles and levels of preparation required for professionals working with young children to provide high-quality services. It must also recognize that individuals enter the profession with diverse educational qualifications and experience and promote a system that encourages ongoing professional development for individuals at all levels and in all roles. The framework must also set high standards for professional performance and distinguish the specialized skills and knowledge of the early childhood profession from those of other professions.

This framework uses the symbol of a *lattice* to communicate the necessary combination of diversity and uniqueness (Bredekamp & Willer, 1992). A career lattice provides for the multiple roles and settings within the early childhood profession (vertical strands), each allowing for steps of greater preparation tied to increased responsibility and compensation within that role/setting (horizontal levels), and allows for movement across roles (diagonals). Each strand of the lattice is interconnected; all strands are a part of the larger entity (the early childhood profession).

The lattice distinguishes the *early childhood field* from the *early childhood profession*. The *field* includes anyone engaged in the provision of early childhood services; the *profession* denotes those who have acquired some professional knowledge and are on a professional path. A professional path requires (1) completion of or enrollment in a credit-bearing early childhood professional preparation program that meets recognized guidelines *or* (2) ongoing participation in formal training that may not be credit bearing but is designed to lead to the acquisition of competency that could be assessed through mechanisms such as the Child Development Associate (CDA) Credential and/or transformed into credit toward another professional credential or degree.

Individuals may be employed in early childhood settings prior to acquiring a recognized professional credential or degree but should work under supervision or with support. Direct, daily supervision may not be feasible for family child care providers who are self-employed and often work alone or with an assistant. Ongoing support and mentoring of family child care providers can be provided through alternative means, such as linkages with a provider association, network, or Child Care Food Program sponsor to identify qualified, experienced providers to serve as mentors.

It is the responsibility of the early childhood profession to define how it uniquely differs from all other professions. A defining characteristic of any profession is a specialized body of knowledge and competencies shared by all of its members that are not shared by others. Although a complete description of the early childhood knowledge and competency base is beyond the scope of this document, it is possible to identify two key questions that can be used to determine its parameters. First, *Is this*

The lattice of early childhood professional development

The common knowledge and abilities shared by all early childhood professionals

NAEYC's leadership has been especially important in defining quality standards for programs for young children.

knowledge or skill required of **every** early childhood professional, regardless of level or setting or professional role? Does every childhood professional need to know and be able to do this in order to effectively practice?

The second question that must be answered is, *Does the sum of this body of knowledge and competencies uniquely distinguish the early childhood professional from all other professionals?* For example, if the core stressed human development through the life span rather than child development, it would define a "human service" professional rather than an "early childhood" professional. This is not to say that no other professionals will share certain areas of knowledge (e.g., child development) but that the sum of the body of knowledge effectively distinguishes early childhood professionals from other professionals. Greater breadth and depth in specific topics beyond the core would be needed in certain specializations (administration and parent education) and at higher levels of professional development. Further discussion of these two questions will lead to greater consensus regarding what knowledge and skills are included in the core versus what are needed for specific roles or levels.

The distinct early childhood core is also revealed by a comparison of common elements in the guidelines for early childhood professional preparation programs, including the Child Development Associate Professional Preparation Program (Phillips, 1991a, 1991b) and NAEYC's guidelines for basic and advanced early childhood professional preparation (1985; 1991). The common elements define what all early childhood professionals must know and be able to do, including:

- demonstrate an understanding of **child development** and apply this knowledge in practice;
- **observe and assess children's behavior** in planning and individualizing teaching practices and curriculum;
- establish and maintain a **safe and healthy environment** for children;
- **plan and implement developmentally appropriate curriculum** that advances all areas of children's learning and development, including social, emotional, intellectual, and physical competence;
- establish supportive relationships with children and implement developmentally appropriate techniques of **guidance and group management**;
- establish and maintain positive and productive **relationships with families**;
- support the development and learning of individual children, recognizing that children are best understood in the context of **family, culture, and society**; and
- demonstrate an understanding of the early childhood profession and make a commitment to **professionalism**.

To effectively implement these common themes, all early childhood professionals need some general knowledge and competencies associated with the full early childhood age span (infants/toddlers, preschoolers, and

All early childhood professionals need some general knowledge and competencies associated with the full early childhood age span.

primary school-agers), including children with special developmental and learning needs, and usually have greater depth of knowledge and experience in two of the three early childhood age groups (infants/toddlers, preschoolers, and primary school-agers). Practicum or work experience under qualified supervision is essential to gaining requisite professional knowledge and skills; NAEYC preparation and teacher certification guidelines recommend supervised experience working with a minimum of two of the three early childhood age groups (NAEYC, 1985, 1991; ATE & NAEYC, 1991).

In addition to working with young children, early childhood professionals must be able to establish and maintain productive relationships with colleagues, work effectively as a member of an instructional team, communicate effectively with parents or other family members, and communicate effectively with other professionals and agencies concerned with children and families in the larger community to support children's development, learning, and well-being.

The early childhood common core deepens and expands with specializations at higher levels of preparation.

The early childhood common core deepens and expands with specializations at higher levels of preparation. An individual successfully completing the CDA Credential has demonstrated competency to meet the specific needs of children and to work with parents and other adults to nurture children's physical, social, emotional, and intellectual growth in a child development framework (Phillips, 1991a, 1991b). At the associate level, the graduate demonstrates technical knowledge and skills necessary to perform competently with a group of children on a daily basis; at the baccalaureate level, the graduate demonstrates the ability to apply and analyze the core knowledge and to systematically plan and develop curriculum for individual children and groups; at the master's level, the graduate demonstrates greater capacity to analyze and refine the core knowledge and evaluate and apply research to improve practices; at the doctoral level, the graduate conducts research and studies practices to expand the knowledge base and influence systems' change. At each of these levels, the professional is expected to engage in reflective practice that contributes to continuing professional development. In addition, at each of these levels, the professional is expected to advocate for policies designed to improve conditions for children, families, and the profession.

In addition to the expanding core of professional knowledge, higher levels of professional development are linked to higher levels of general education. Linking general education and professional development is important for at least three reasons. First, research suggests that the breadth of knowledge associated with college education is related to quality for children (Whitebook, Howes, & Phillips, 1989). Second, general knowledge constitutes the "content" of the curriculum for children. Children want and need to learn about everything—science, social studies, literature, math, music, and everything else in their world of experience. To provide experiences that reflect this broad content requires knowledgeable teachers. Third, a crucial interaction occurs between professional knowledge and general knowledge; at higher levels, professional knowledge is embedded within an increasingly broader context. This broader context means that early childhood concepts are informed by the application of knowledge from other disciplines, and it helps to generate new knowledge.

General education and specialized professional education are automatically linked for individuals who complete formal preparation programs, especially those that meet NAEYC's guidelines. Some, but far from all, practitioners complete a professional preparation program before formally working in the field. Many others enter the early childhood professional path later in their careers. Sometimes they have already acquired a college degree in another field before deciding to work with young children; sometimes their experiences working in the early childhood field or as parents convince them to seek professional training. Barriers—lack of money, scheduling problems, limited availability or accessibility of programs, institutional racism, a mismatch between language or literacy expectations and skills—have made it difficult for many practitioners to pursue professional preparation. These issues can and must be redressed. Strategies such as scholarships and financial aid, transforming mechanisms to grant credit for knowledge and competencies gained through experiential learning, and meaningful increases in compensation linked to the completion of a preparation program and improved performance will enhance the likelihood that more individuals will complete recognized preparation programs.

A number of states and communities are beginning to develop comprehensive career development plans.

The table on page 16 identifies six levels of early professional development, beginning with those just starting on a professional path. This system of levels is based on the expected outcomes of the various levels of preparation programs. It is designed to reflect a continuum of professional development. The defined steps reflect programs of study for which nationally recognized standards have been set. Not identified as separate levels but implicit in the notion of a continuum are training programs based on the early childhood core that are designed to recognize the acquisition of knowledge or competencies prior to completion of a nationally recognized credential or degree; for example, the military child care system offers training modules designed to lead to acquisition of a CDA Credential.

Currently, community-based training is rarely linked to formal credit and therefore cannot be used toward the next degree (Morgan et al., 1993). A number of states and communities are beginning to develop comprehensive career development plans that create transformation mechanisms allowing individuals to demonstrate their knowledge and competencies and receive credit toward a recognized degree. In addition, the trend toward outcome-based teacher education, promoted by the National Council for Accreditation in Teacher Education (NCATE) and

This table is designed to reflect a continuum of professional development. The levels identify levels of preparation programs for which standards have been established nationally.

Table 1. Definitions of Early Childhood
Professional Categories

Early Childhood Professional Level VI

Successful completion of a Ph.D. or Ed.D. in a program conforming to NAEYC guidelines; OR

Successful demonstration of the knowledge, performance, and dispositions expected as outcomes of a doctoral degree program conforming to NAEYC guidelines.

Early Childhood Professional Level V

Successful completion of a master's degree in a program that conforms to NAEYC guidelines; OR

Successful demonstration of the knowledge, performance, and dispositions expected as outcomes of a master's degree program conforming to NAEYC guidelines.

Early Childhood Professional Level IV

Successful completion of a baccalaureate degree from a program conforming to NAEYC guidelines; OR

State certificate meeting NAEYC certification guidelines; OR

Successful completion of a baccalaureate degree in another field with more than 30 professional units in early childhood development/education including 300 hours of supervised teaching experience, including 150 hours each for two of the following three age groups: infants and toddlers, 3- to 5-year-olds, or the primary grades; OR

Successful demonstration of the knowledge, performance, and dispositions expected as outcomes of a baccalaureate degree program conforming to NAEYC guidelines.

Early Childhood Professional Level III

Successful completion of an associate degree from a program conforming to NAEYC guidelines; OR

Successful completion of an associate degree in a related field, plus 30 units of professional studies in early childhood development/education including 300 hours of supervised teaching experience in an early childhood program; OR

Successful demonstration of the knowledge, performance, and dispositions expected as outcomes of an associate degree program conforming to NAEYC guidelines.

Early Childhood Professional Level II

II. B. Successful completion of a one-year early childhood certificate program.

II. A. Successful completion of the CDA Professional Preparation Program OR completion of a systematic, comprehensive training program that prepares an individual to successfully acquire the CDA Credential through direct assessment.

Early Childhood Professional Level I

Individuals who are employed in an early childhood professional role working under supervision or with support (e.g., linkages with provider association or network or enrollment in supervised practicum) and participating in training designed to lead to the assessment of individual competencies or acquisition of a degree.

performance-based licensure systems emerging in states throughout the nation, stresses what knowledge, performances, and dispositions must be demonstrated rather than specifying one invariant route presumed to lead to their acquisition. Alternative approaches to gain and demonstrate competency already exist at the level of the CDA. Individuals may acquire the CDA by completing the CDA Professional Preparation Program or through direct assessment.

Many roles exist within the early childhood profession, and these roles exist within a variety of settings. Roles vary in the specific knowledge, competencies, and levels of education that are required; differences may also exist by setting. The process of developing consensus regarding the specific expectations of knowledge and skills needed in different roles and settings is underway. Many of the areas of specialization within the early childhood field (i.e., family child care providers, directors, regulators, resource and referral) are defining the specific competencies and systems needed for their roles.

Expectations of knowledge and competencies in different roles

Just as there are common themes of knowledge and abilities that transcend the various levels, roles, and settings within the early childhood profession, there are also common themes related to ensuring an effective process of professional development regardless of level, role, or setting. Detailing a full description of effective professional development processes is beyond the scope of this document. The following principles have been extrapolated from research on effective professional development (Epstein, 1993; Modigliani, 1993).

Principles of effective professional development

　　1. Professional development is an ongoing process.

　　All early childhood professionals—no matter how qualified—need to continue to incorporate into their professional repertoire new knowledge and skills related to working with young children and their families. NAEYC recommends that all early childhood professionals complete 24 clock hours of ongoing professional development each year.

　　2. Professional development experiences are most effective when grounded in a sound theoretical and philosophical base and structured as a coherent and systematic program.

　　Currently, many early childhood practitioners, particularly those who have not completed formal preparation programs, gain training through a scatter-shot approach that often reflects their state's child care licensing requirements or the availability of training opportunities at a given time. A scatter-shot approach makes it difficult to integrate and apply new information and often results in duplication of some topics and gaps in others.

　　3. Professional development experiences are most successful when they respond to individuals' background, experiences, and the current context of their role.

This principle is particularly important for employed individuals who are often investing scarce resources—both time and money—in training and may feel cheated or frustrated when there are few apparent links to their needs. Such congruence is particularly important in the beginning stages of professional development because it is more difficult to make connections on one's own without a broad foundation of knowledge and skills.

Effective professional development experiences provide opportunities for application and reflection.

4. Effective professional development opportunities are structured to promote clear linkages between theory and practice.

Without clear linkages between theory and practice, students may reject new knowledge as "book learning" or an "ivory tower" approach and instead rely on experienced practitioners' information and strategies "that work in the real world."

5. Providers of effective professional development experiences have an appropriate knowledge and experience base.

In addition to helping to ensure the accuracy and quality of the material presented, meeting this principle is important for establishing credibility and legitimacy in the eyes of the participants.

6. Effective professional development experiences use an active, hands-on approach and stress an interactive approach that encourages students to learn from one another.

In addition to reflecting what is known about effective strategies for teaching adults, meeting this principle has the added benefit of modeling the same type of teaching practices that are effective when working with young children.

7. Effective professional development experiences contribute to positive self-esteem by acknowledging the skills and resources brought to the training process as opposed to creating feelings of self-doubt or inadequacy by immediately calling into question an individual's current practices.

The low pay and status of many individuals working with young children already works to undermine practitioners' self-esteem, which in turn can have negative effects on their interactions with young children. Additionally, building upon existing strengths makes it more likely that the new information will be incorporated into the individual's repertoire, and the opposite approach is likely to result in the rejection of new information ("You don't know my kids; that would never work with them").

8. Effective professional development experiences provide opportunities for application and reflection and allow for individuals to be observed and receive feedback upon what has been learned.

Learning is most clearly integrated into an individual's professional repertoire when there are frequent opportunities to utilize the new information, to reflect upon its meaning and applications, and to receive feedback on how the new knowledge or skill is incorporated into one's practice. Isolated, one-shot training experiences do not provide for such integration and reflection, nor do formal preparation programs that teach theoretical foundations early on without any practicum experiences until much later.

9. Students and professionals should be involved in the planning and design of their professional development program.

Meeting this principle helps to ensure that the professional development experiences are tailored to meet individual needs. It also encourages individuals to develop a stronger sense of ownership for their learning and reinforces the notion that professional development is an ongoing professional responsibility.

Linking professional development and compensation

There is little incentive for pursuing a system of differentiated professional qualifications unless increased qualifications are rewarded with improved compensation. The following guidelines are designed to link increased professional development with improved compensation. It is recognized that some early childhood programs will require additional resources before these guidelines can be fully implemented. Families alone cannot be expected to bear the additional costs. NAEYC is committed to working for strategies that acknowledge the full cost of quality early childhood program provision and that distribute these costs more equitably among all sectors of society. NAEYC believes that parents and early childhood professionals have borne a disproportionate burden in the provision of early childhood programs. All of society—children, families, employers, communities, and the nation as a whole—benefits from the provision of high-quality early childhood programs. It is time that the full cost of this essential public service be shared more equitably by all sectors of society.

- **Early childhood professionals with comparable qualifications, experience, and job responsibilities should receive comparable compensation regardless of the setting of their job. This means that a teacher working in a community child care center, a family child care provider, and an elementary school teacher who each hold comparable professional qualifications and carry out comparable functions or responsibilities should also receive comparable compensation for their work.**

Early childhood professionals who work directly with young children typically are employed in a variety of settings including public schools; part-day and full-day centers, whether for-profit or nonprofit; public and private prekindergarten programs, including Head Start; before- and after-school programs; and family child care. Despite the differences in setting, the nature of the job responsibilities is generally similar.

Although the work of all early childhood professionals has been undervalued, those professionals working with children in situations other than serving school-age children during the traditional school day have been the most undercompensated. For example, a recent national study

Early childhood professionals who have comparable qualifications and job responsibilities should also receive comparable compensation.

(U.S. GAO, 1989) found that teachers in early childhood programs accredited by NAEYC earned roughly half that of their counterparts in public schools, holding education and experience constant. Even within the public school, salaries have been found to be depressed for equally qualified teachers of preschool children, especially when program funding is based on parent fees or special program subsidies (Mitchell & Modigliani, 1989). As a matter of equity, early childhood professionals who have comparable qualifications and job responsibilities should also receive comparable compensation.

- **Compensation for early childhood professionals should be equivalent to that of other professionals with comparable preparation requirements, experience, and job responsibilities.**

Although removing disparity within the early childhood profession is an important step forward, given the undervaluing of all work with young children, it is an insufficient goal. Early childhood salary schedules and benefits should be determined following a review of salary schedules for members of other professional groups. Reviews should be conducted within the community and, when feasible, within the early childhood program's larger organizational structure.

Although an institutional review may not be feasible for small independent programs, it has proven to be an effective tool for improving compensation in many programs associated with a larger institution. The institutional review is an internal review, considering salaries and benefits provided to individuals with similar preparation and responsibilities. For example, a community service organization may compare the salaries and benefits of its early childhood teaching staff to its social workers with equivalent preparation and responsibility. A public school would examine the comparability of responsibilities and preparation and corresponding compensation for teachers in its prekindergarten and kindergarten programs to secondary teachers. The compensation of a program administrator in an organization such as a hospital, industry, or educational institution would be compared to the compensation package of heads of other programs or departments of similar size within that institution.

The community review, possible for all programs, should begin by considering professionals with similar responsibilities. The job responsibilities of early childhood professionals are most comparable to those of other educational professionals in elementary and secondary schools. The community review should also take into account other professionals in the community. These may include nurses, social workers, and counselors as well as others. Many of the social services share with the early childhood profession in the undervaluing of their work; broader comparability to more equitably paid professions should be the long-term goal.

It should be noted that family child care providers are typically not salaried employees, but are self-employed with income based on fees for service. Community reviews may provide useful information for family child care providers when determining fees. Fees should be based on the full cost of providing a high-quality service and include sufficient compensation for the level of professional preparation.

- **Compensation should not be differentiated on the basis of the ages of children served.**

Assuming equivalent professional preparation and equivalent job responsibilities, early childhood professionals working with young children should receive compensation comparable to professionals working with older children. Typically, the younger the child, the lesser the value placed on the service provided. Yet, children are most vulnerable in their early years, and the impact of their early experiences on later development and learning is the most profound. Compensation provided to individuals working with young children should reflect the importance of their work.

Compensation provided to individuals working with young children should reflect the importance of their work.

- **Early childhood professionals should be encouraged to seek additional professional preparation and should be rewarded accordingly.**

Currently there is little incentive for early childhood personnel to seek additional training. Despite the lack of public understanding as to its importance, specialized knowledge of how young children develop and learn is the key predictor of how well early childhood personnel are able to implement a developmentally appropriate program (Bredekamp, 1989). Even when individuals understand the importance of professional development for improving the quality of early childhood services, access to continuing education is often denied due to a lack of resources.

The current crisis in recruiting and retaining qualified staff has resulted in many programs employing individuals who are underqualified for their roles and responsibilities. The provision of in-service training is especially critical in these situations so that children receive the quality of care they need. When the acquisition of additional preparation is not rewarded, there is little incentive for these individuals to remain on the job and the investment made in their in-service training is lost.

- **The provision of an adequate benefits package is a crucial component of compensation for early childhood staff.**

Early childhood personnel who are satisfied with their jobs and whose individual and family members' health is protected are more likely to convey positive feelings toward children, are more able to give utmost attention to teaching and caring for children, and are more likely to remain in their positions for longer periods of time. Benefits packages for full-time staff may be negotiated to meet individual staff members' needs but should include paid leave (annual, sick, and/or personal), medical insurance, and retirement and may provide educational benefits, subsidized child care, or other options unique to the situation. Benefits for part-time staff should be provided on a prorated basis. (Students or others who are placed on the job on a temporary basis for job-training purposes are excluded from this provision.)

- **Career ladders should be established, providing additional increments in salary based on performance and participation in professional development opportunities.**

Individuals who work directly with young children should be able to envision a future in this work. Too often, the only opportunity for advancement in early childhood programs requires leaving direct work with children. Career ladders linked to a salary scale offer opportunities for advancement through merit increases and recognition of higher levels of preparation and mastery of practice. By offering opportunities for advancement while continuing to work with children, career ladders promote higher quality services for children.

Salary scales typically include professional qualifications as one of many factors (Bloom, 1993a, 1993b). Other factors—such as job responsibility and performance and local economic factors including compensation in comparable occupations—also need to be considered when making specific salary determinations.

Conclusion

This conceptual framework reflects the current state of professional knowledge and experience as well as input from hundreds of early childhood educators reflecting the diverse roles, backgrounds, and settings of the early childhood profession. It is intended as a working tool designed to promote a coordinated, articulated system of high-quality early childhood professional preparation and development. This document is viewed as a dynamic statement that will be revised based on need and as new knowledge is acquired concerning the education of young children and the preparation of the adults who work with them.

References

Association of Teacher Educators and National Association for the Education of Young Children (ATE & NAEYC). (1991). Early childhood teacher certification. *Young Children, 47*(1), 16–21.

Bloom, P.J. (1993a). Full cost of quality report. "But I'm worth more than that!": Addressing employee concerns about compensation. *Young Children, 48*(3), 65–68.

Bloom, P.J. (1993b). Full cost of quality report. "But I'm worth more than that!": Implementing a comprehensive compensation system. *Young Children, 48*(4), 67–72.

Bredekamp, S. (1989). *Regulating child care quality: Evidence from NAEYC's accreditation system.* Washington, DC: NAEYC.

Bredekamp, S., & Willer, B. (1992). Of ladders and lattices, cores and cones: Conceptualizing an early childhood professional development system. *Young Children, 47*(3), 47–50.

Epstein, A.S. (1993). *Training for quality: Improving early childhood programs through systematic inservice training.* Monographs of the High/Scope Educational Research Foundation, Number Nine. Ypsilanti, MI: High/Scope Educational Research Foundation.

Galinsky, E., Shubilla, L., Willer, B., Levine, J., & Daniel, J. (1994). State and community planning for early childhood systems. *Young Children, 49*(2), 54–57.

Kagan, S.L., & the *Quality 2000* Essentials Task Force. (1994). Essential functions of the early care and education system: Rationale and definition. New Haven, CT: *Quality 2000* Initiative.

Melaville, A.I., Blank, M.J., & Asayesh, G. (1993). Together we can: A guide for crafting a profamily system of education and human services. Washington, DC: U.S. Government Printing Office.

Mitchell, A., & Modigliani, K. (1989). Public policy report. Young children in the public schools? The "only ifs" reconsidered. *Young Children, 44*(6), 56–61.

Modigliani, K. (1993). Readings in family child care professional development: Project-to-project compiled. Boston, MA: Wheelock College Family Child Care Project.

Morgan, G., Azer, S., Costley, J., Genser, A., Goodman, I., Lombardi, J., & McGimsey, B. (1993). *Making a career of it: The state of the states report on career development in early care and education.* Boston, MA: The Center for Career Development in Early Care and Education at Wheelock College.

National Association for the Education of Young Children (NAEYC). (1985). *Guidelines for early childhood education programs in associate degree granting institutions.* Washington, DC: Author.

National Association for the Education of Young Children (NAEYC). (1991). *Early childhood teacher education guidelines: Basic and advanced.* Washington, DC: Author.

National Association of State Boards of Education (NASBE). (1991). *Caring communities: Supporting young children and families. The report of the National Task Force on School Readiness.* Alexandria, VA: Author.

Phillips, C.B. (Ed.). (1991a). *Essentials for Child Development Associates working with young children.* Washington, DC: Council for Early Childhood Professional Recognition.

Phillips, C.B. (Ed.). (1991b). *Field advisor's guide for the CDA Professional Preparation Program.* Washington, DC: Council for Early Childhood Professional Recognition.

U.S. General Accounting Office (GAO). (1989). *Early childhood education: Information on costs and services at high quality centers.* Washington, DC: Author.

Whitebook, M., Howes, C., & Phillips, D. (1989). *Who cares? Child care teachers and the quality of care in America.* Final report of the National Child Care Staffing Study. Oakland, CA: Child Care Employee Project.

Willer, B., Hofferth, S., Kisker, E., Divine-Hawkins, P., Farquhar, E., & Glantz, F. (1991). *The demand and supply of child care in 1990: Joint findings from the National Child Care Survey 1990 and A Profile of Child Care Settings.* Washington, DC: NAEYC.

PART I

Paths from the Field: Toward a Profession

Few professions are as complex as early childhood education. Individuals enter the field's career lattice from various directions and at many different points. Paths on the lattice are characterized by varying work and educational experiences. All routes, however, are paved with the strength of a common knowledge base.

An honest look at the profession reveals very real inequities in status, differing standards for programs and practitioners, countless program delivery mechanisms, and a lack of consensus on cherished values. Systematizing professional development can be achieved only when these challenges are addressed and resolved.

Elizabeth Jones breaks the ice by confronting the issue of professional status. Her expertise in facilitating professional development and teaching human development courses at Pacific Oaks College enables her to penetrate the haze across the field. She uses one community's experience to demonstrate the incongruity between teacher credentials, status, pay, and levels of quality of programs and services for young children, and sets the stage for an open, frank discussion of issues that impinge on the vision of professional preparation.

A related and yet different vantage point is explored by **Cheryl-Ann Whitehead.** Family child care providers—who serve about half of the chil-

Paths on the lattice are characterized by varying work and educational experiences.

dren in child care—are an essential partner in the consensus-building process and must be included in a comprehensive model of professional development. Whitehead, president of Windflower and a consultant specializing in family child care, cites the unique qualities and family-centered approach that family child care brings to the career lattice.

Additional obstacles and paths within the profession are described by **Betty L. Hutchison,** a faculty member at National-Louis University. She recognizes the lack of articulation between standards, training, and program delivery, all three of which are components of a sound professional development system. Her vision lays a foundation upon which to incorporate these components.

Gwen Morgan, founder of The Center for Career Development in Early Care and Education at Wheelock College, acknowledges these and many other competing concerns in the quest for professionalism. She outlines a dynamic model that reconciles some of these issues, offers many advantages, and enables the field to move ahead.

A sense of urgency is conveyed by **Jan McCarthy,** a former NAEYC president and a veteran teacher educator who is also a former president of the National Council for Accreditation of Teacher Education (NCATE). She reviews the evolving challenges for professionals, the detrimental effects of the lack of professional standards, and the promising benefits of state/NCATE partnerships and outcome-based teacher preparation.

Breaking the Ice: Confronting Status Differences among Professionals

Elizabeth Jones

Early childhood educators face the challenge of establishing standards for professional preparation while avoiding the elitism evident in many traditional fields. NAEYC, by its open membership policy, has always recognized the great pool of experience-based competence in early childhood education. We continue to struggle to articulate informal and formal learning in order to provide genuine access to professional development for a highly diverse group of people. Rarely have human beings been very good at creative resolution of conflicts that arise out of their differences. People are much more apt to mark their territory and then fight for it. Animals mark their territory by "peeing" on it; birds, by singing about it. Professionals mark theirs by writing professional standards.

As participants in a continuing partnership between Pacific Oaks College and a public school district's early childhood programs, several colleagues and I have observed firsthand a territorial struggle that exemplifies the issues of professionalism faced in many communities. The following case study takes place in a California city of 120,000 people within a large multiethnic, multilingual metropolitan area.

Staking out the territory

In this community, a half-dozen different publicly funded programs serve low-income 3- and 4-year-olds. Head Start and a small state preschool program are administered by private nonprofit agencies. Four other programs are administered by the public school district:

1. State children's centers, operating since the 1940s, offer full-day child care.

2. State preschools, established around 1970, offer half-day programs serving the same population as Head Start. Children's centers and state preschools report to the District's Children's Services Office and have had low visibility and status.

3. Preschool special education programs are integrated in part with state preschools.

4. Kindergarten for 4-year-olds, established in 1989 with private foundation funds and serving the same population as state preschools, was designed to integrate preschools into the public elementary schools. A K-4 program was placed in every public school and staffed with a credentialed teacher who reported to the school principal and was defined as a member of the school faculty. K-4 was new, different, and well-publicized. In its third year of operation, the local newspaper reported that the program had been shown to be superior to Head Start and state preschools.

As is often the case, most of the grant funding for K-4 ended after three years. However, the timely availability of state preschool expansion funds made it possible for the K-4 program to merge with the state preschools.

Who teaches 4-year-olds best? A case study

The school district now has 22 state preschools with morning and afternoon classes, each staffed with 2 teachers and a teacher's aide. Among the 44 teachers in the merged program, some have elementary credentials. A few have special education credentials. The rest have children's center permits, which are based on an associate degree or beyond and are required for state preschools. Permit teachers have diverse backgrounds; some have been in charge of their own classrooms for years while others who were formerly K-4 assistants have only recently completed minimum permit requirements to qualify them as teachers.

Although both types of teachers do the same job, the credentialed teachers can earn twice the salary of permit teachers, even those teachers with many years of experience. Predictably, in a district where only 20% of public school enrollment is Anglo, the majority of the credentialed teachers are Anglo. The majority of the permit teachers, and nearly all classroom aides, are people of color.

As we have observed informally in these preschool classrooms, we see that some teaching teams work together collaboratively, some appear comfortable with a hierarchy in which the credentialed teacher is in charge, and some are painfully hierarchical, characterized by an assumption of superior status by the credentialed teacher. As we have looked for developmentally appropriate practice—with emphasis on play, language development, and relationships with families—we have observed that some teachers define their program in these terms. Others, consciously or not, define the preschool program as orientation to school, with indicators such as calendar, flag salute, teacher-directed language and craft projects, and lunch in the school cafeteria. Some programs genuinely include families in classroom planning and activities; others seem to patronize them. Credentialed teachers are somewhat more likely than permit teachers to define their task in orientation-to-school terms, but this is not consistent.

From this case study, six points emerge for consideration in discussions about professionalism for the field of early childhood education.

1. **The type of credential, in the setting described, is not predictive of program quality.** Teachers with different credentials provide high- and lower-quality programs for children and families. Our informal observations do not confirm the claims of superiority of the K-4 program.

2. **The type of credential held is predictive of salary, ethnicity, social class background, and status within the system as perceived by self and others.** Taken together, these factors correlate with teachers' assertiveness in the face of opposition, although there are certainly exceptions. Teachers who grew up in positions of social power are likely to assume their "rightness" in professional practice.

3. **Teachers who "play school," rather than seriously support children's play as a vehicle for learning, have a status edge with elementary colleagues, many principals, and many families, especially within the public school setting.** Individuals in this higher-status group hold a vision of what "real school" looks like—teachers instruct in groups, and children produce uniform work—and are reassured to see these strategies duplicated in preschool. Experienced teachers who model developmentally appropriate practice but lack elementary credentials, have trouble defending their philosophy in the face of such pressure. They are not considered to be "real teachers" by public school definition.

4. **The confident behaviorism and additional-credential status of special education teachers (there are half a dozen inclusion classes in the program) add another level to the status hierarchy.** These teachers are typically viewed as specialists whose knowledge (represented by their credential) about the unique needs of a select group of children is rarely questioned.

5. **Preschool programs administered by a separate children's services department in a school district are likely to remain peripheral and invisible.** Such a structure does, however, build in the possibility of consistent support for developmentally appropriate practice, which is rare when preschool teachers report to building principals.

6. **People in positions of power take the existing system for granted.** In any system, Delpit (1988) points out, those with higher status are least likely to be aware of, and are least willing to acknowledge, inequities in status and power. Those with less power are often most aware of its existence. Credentialed teachers, as well as administrators and union representatives, assume from their own experience that anyone who wants the perks of higher status should get the credential. This generally unspoken attitude reflects one of the major risks of professionalism: distance from clients (children and families) and from colleagues all along the career lattice. This distance often results in patronizing some people and excluding others.

Moving toward solutions

This story's moral is consistent with the goals for appropriate practice with children. Tender topics—such as status inequities—can and must be talked about. Only when the ice is broken on the topic of professional status can the field move away from the less-than-inclusive status quo. But talking is not easy in settings where professional behavior is defined as keeping negative feelings to oneself, not airing them in public.

When I proposed collective storytelling as the agenda for an in-service early childhood meeting at the end of the merger year, the staff development coordinator was skeptical. I persisted, explaining that people were experiencing program changes as losses to be mourned. Structural realities can cause frustration and anger. Confronting the issues can result in less blaming of each other and movement toward common solutions. The coordinator agreed to try it.

Because I am outside the system with some credibility in it as a facilitator, I began by telling the story of the year, inviting others to add to it. When the racial difference between credentialed and permit teachers was mentioned, a White teacher who is dependably a risk-taker blurted out, "When you say people of color, you are implying that I am colorless, and I resent that. These differences don't really matter." The discussion became a lot more lively after that, and we moved from the large group to small groups to continue it.

By acknowledging negative feelings and naming their structural sources, we make dialogue possible. By publicly naming the issues that those in power habitually do not acknowledge (and may not even understand), we open the way for those with less power but greater understanding to speak out with authority about their personal experiences with inequity. Good teachers encourage children to use words to confront unfairness and create solutions to conflicts. Early childhood teachers' encounters with other adults are just as important professionally as their encounters with children.

In a study conducted at a community college, Oberg (1992) found that early childhood teachers' own priority for their continued learning was "skills and knowledge in relating to others, both adults and children. . . . This emphasis on connections between people is very different from the content and organization of traditional teacher training programs" (p. 43). Connections between people aren't only psychological; they are also cultural and political. Most cultures are sustained by a heavy dose of mystery—rules for things we don't talk about. Although this is a useful strategy to sustain tradition, it gets in the way of clear thinking about social change. Like it or not, the early childhood profession's challenge is to change things. By naming our experiences, and acknowledging the social contexts in which they occur, teachers and children can become competent change-makers.

Bibliography/ Resources

Delpit, L. (1988, August). The silenced dialogue: Power and pedagogy in educating other people's children. *Harvard Educational Review, 58*(3), 280–298.

Jones, E. (Ed.). (1993). *Growing teachers: Partnerships in staff development.* Washington, DC: NAEYC.

Oberg, K. (1992). *Reaching child care teachers: When experience precedes education* (occasional paper). Pasadena, CA: Pacific Oaks College.

Seeking Common Ground: The Family Child Care Perspective

Cheryl-Ann Whitehead

In the not-too-distant past, family child care was unregulated and invisible. Providers were unconnected and isolated. They were usually referred to as baby-sitters and viewed as simply custodial caregivers. As child care regulations were established in all but a few states, the image of family child care as a professional service began to emerge.

The United States Department of Agriculture's Child Care Food Program stirred some of the first organizational feelings of family child care providers by bringing them together for educational workshops. As providers met and shared experiences, they began to form local support groups. Out of these early contacts in states including Colorado, Washington, and New York, a few of today's oldest, most established provider associations were formed. Family child care as an entity within the field of early childhood education was still hard to identify, but with time providers slowly found each other.

Family child care is more visible and recognized than ever before but there is still a long way to go.

More recently, the visibility of family child care increased at an incredible rate, due in large part to the proliferation of child care resource and referral (R & R) agencies. As R & Rs formed across the country, family child care was swept along, particularly as parents demanded family child care. Through the connection of parents to family child care, R & Rs recognized many of the unmet needs of providers. R & Rs began to support providers, meet their needs, and enhance service quality. The message was soon carried to funders and other interested parties.

One major effort, the Family-to-Family Project funded by the Dayton Hudson Foundation, which was administered first through Mervyn's and then Target Stores, grew out of these early advocacy efforts on behalf of family child care. The initiative boosted the visibility and positive image of family child care in many cities across the country by investing in provider education and recognition (see Part III, Cohen & Modigliani, of this volume).

At the same time, family child care became more organized in its own right. State and local associations blossomed throughout the country as providers discovered the joy of coming together with their peers, breaking the isolation, supporting each other, and sharing pride in their work. The trend continues with new associations forming and growing daily. In 1993, the National Association for Family Day Care (NAFDC) marked its 10th anniversary and changed its name to the National Association for Family Child Care.

The process of giving birth to a profession is still underway as associations continue to evolve and more providers enter the regulatory system. Family child care is more visible and recognized than ever before. However, there is still a long way to go.

Toward visibility and unity

Think about the number of times during the past year that a magazine or newspaper article, or a TV news or special report, featured child care. Of all the articles or reports, how many mentioned or even acknowledged the existence of family child care? Despite the number of children in family child care—nearly half of the children in all child care settings—the media tend to focus on center-based care.

Political power and high visibility undoubtedly are among the reasons for this emphasis. Center-based programs have more clout and visibility; family child care homes do not. This is understandable because center-based care was organized long before family child care.

Although NAEYC is nearly 70 years old and has about 90,000 members, family child care has not been proportionately represented within the membership. Quite naturally, as NAEYC became a stronger voice for the field, advocacy efforts leaned toward the majority of the Association's center-based members. This is changing, as family child care providers attend NAEYC conferences along with other early childhood professionals.

Family child care also faces racism and elitism. The prejudice and discrimination directed at family child care, from within the field of early

Teaching may not look or happen the same way it does in other settings because the natural learning environment is so much a part of family child care.

childhood education, is often incredibly subtle and difficult to address openly. Discrimination, however, does exist. Some individuals, leaders, and organizations would, if given the choice, eliminate family child care. Others see family child care as a special interest group within the broader early childhood profession, implying that family child care is only a small part of the whole. Statistics tell us otherwise. The saying, "Just because you're paranoid doesn't mean they're not out to get you," comes to mind. The derogatory attitudes, prejudices, and stereotypes must be brought into the open, with awareness that each exists due to the lack of understanding and knowledge about family child care and what it has to offer.

The lack of visibility and political unity of family child care has also hindered the ability to break through the myth that providers do not teach. Teaching may not look or happen the same way it does in other settings because the natural learning environment is so much a part of family child care. Providers do in fact teach in developmentally appropriate ways, and children do learn.

When each of these challenges are considered, it is no wonder that the media fail to acknowledge or value family child care. In overlooking family child care's long-standing contribution to families and the field, the future of the profession is negatively affected. Parents and policymakers absorb the not-so-subtle message that the best, or most acceptable, child care is what is most often talked about—center-based care.

Early childhood educators must recognize that many parents prefer family child care, and not just because it may be cheaper or because it serves infants and toddlers! Family child care deserves equal partner status, with a rightful place and in proportionate numbers wherever child care issues are discussed. Inviting one provider who claims to support the family child care perspective is shortsighted and a disservice to the field.

Becoming professional partners

Family child care is still struggling to organize and to decide how it defines professionalism in a way that builds on providers' special qualities. In the midst of all these challenges, providers are keeping pace with the movement to articulate a model for professional development. The many dedicated, qualified, knowledgeable family child care providers must be included in this model.

Family child care providers are not going to take their marbles and go home; nor will they throw their marbles at others in the field. Providers hope to help other early childhood professionals understand and appreciate providers and their contributions. They seek to be included in a way that retains their unique qualities. As one provider stated at an NAEYC Annual Conference Membership Expression of Opinion session, family child care "holds up half of the sky" in this field.

> Another reason that family day care has been discovered is that, like many of the explorers coming to a new land, there are those who would like to change the service into something that is more familiar (like preschools or

Family child care deserves equal partner status, with a rightful place and in proportionate numbers wherever child care issues are discussed.

day care centers); something that is neater and tidier in terms of record keeping; something that is more controllable. Names have changed: We have rejected the term "baby-sitter," have struggled with family day care mother (or father); have gone to the term caregiver, operator, and provider and there is now a push to be called teacher. Of course, we're all teachers—but we operate in different environments and do different things. It is essential that we maintain these differences, so that there are many options and alternatives for children and families choosing child care. (Sale, 1977)

All early childhood educators are dedicated to providing quality care and education for young children. A model of professional development can be built on this common ground. This vision for the future emerges from the voices and hearts of family child care providers all over the country:

- Family child care will be granted the time, space, and support it deserves to emerge as a profession. Family child care will be respected by experts, policymakers, and the media for what it offers children and families.

- Family child care philosophy will apply to all forms of early childhood education, bringing to life Sale's assertion that "our centers need to be more like our homes" rather than vice versa.

- The early childhood profession will avoid narrow definitions of professionalism, quality services, and how to obtain knowledge and education. It will acknowledge *many right ways* within a framework of acceptable standards and foster options and choices that respect diversity.

- The family child care model of relationships and family focus will be a goal for all early childhood programs. Early childhood professionals protect the nation's future by nurturing ties among children, their families, and caregivers.

- Family child care will achieve its rightful place as an equal partner in the early childhood arena. Experience is validated, not for its own sake, but by virtue of what was learned.

- The profession will work together to create a strong caring community that benefits and supports all its members and, more importantly, the children and families we serve.

Reference

Sale, J.S. (1977). *Family day care organizations: Surviving and thriving.* Paper presented at the meeting of the Great Falls Day Care Association, Great Falls, MT.

Dream or Nightmare? A Vision for Professional Development

Betty L. Hutchison

Efforts to coordinate early childhood professional development must consider the current realities for many people. Students at all levels who have the dream of working with young children soon discover that their dream more closely resembles a nightmare. Consider these three scenarios.

* * *

Scene 1: *I like kids and have a couple of little ones of my own. It's hard to go out to work, so I take a few kids into my home. My state, like most, has just a few licensing standards for family child care providers who take in several children. I'm not required to get any training, but I sure learn a lot each day from the children and their parents. When I do go to workshops, the information is really basic and all those workshops don't count toward anything.*

Family care providers are the nation's largest group of early childhood educators, as Whitehead (this volume) indicates. They accumulate valuable on-the-job experience and knowledge. Not only do their long, lonely, and typically underpaid hours make it difficult to engage in more formal learning experiences, but many local courses and workshops are designed for center-based personnel rather than home-based providers. Often the workshops are repetitive, disjointed, and rarely provide recognized credit.

* * *

Scene 2: *Two years ago, my child was in Head Start. I volunteered at first, and then they offered me a paying job as an aide. I had a high-school diploma. Then I earned a Child Development Associate Credential (CDA) through this new system that made it possible for me to earn some college credit at the same time. The CDA really boosted my confidence, so I'm ready to take the plunge into college so I can become a head teacher or director.*

This teacher may be about to encounter another barrier: CDA credits, which are competency-based, may or may not satisfy very many degree requirements, depending on the institution. Obtaining a CDA and a college degree are very difficult processes and may take more time and money than is available.

* * *

Scene 3: *I didn't have any real career goal in mind because my high-school grades were mediocre. I decided to go to my local community college because it costs less. During my counseling session I uttered these fateful words, "Well, I do like children." Instantly, I was in a child development class. And I loved it! I completed my two-year degree and decided to prepare myself for another rung on the career ladder. Then I found out I have only 15 credits of general education that apply toward a four-year degree.*

Teacher certification is the ultimate goal of most baccalaureate professional programs in early childhood education. Senior-level professional courses are required for certification, and early childhood credits earned at other levels generally do not apply.

These scenes of dreams on their way to becoming nightmares all involve relationships—or the lack thereof—between unrelated training entities. Teacher preparation requirements often differ even within an institution. Individuals seeking certification in special education, elementary education, or early childhood education each pursue different preparation programs. Graduates of each of these programs, however, could conceivably serve the same child, albeit in different ways. Early childhood faculty in four-year teacher training institutions often encounter significant differences with elementary educators and special educators, including priorities, professional affiliations, and definitions of developmentally appropriate practice.

If there is discord *within* the teacher preparation arena, consider the lack of continuity between practitioners of related disciplines who serve young children: recreation specialists, speech therapists, family counselors and therapists, children's librarians, child life specialists, child care licensing staff, resource and referral personnel, and many more. All of these professionals may be as knowledgeable and concerned about appropriate practice and advocacy as early childhood teachers, but clearly do not fit into a professional career lattice defined in educational terms.

Individuals seeking certification in special education, elementary education, or early childhood education each pursue different preparation programs but could conceivably serve the same child.

Suppose the bright and eager two-year college graduate cited earlier decides to work with a resource and referral agency, helping parents locate services or developing community resources. What interdisciplinary program prepares people for these careers that demand knowledge of young children, social service skills, and much more? This is just one example of the lack of fit between current professional preparation structures and the need for practitioners who can provide a variety of important services for young children and their families.

Good early childhood practice traditionally has focused on the child and family, and our efforts have been fruitful. The increasing attention being paid to the quality of preschool programs through such efforts as the accreditation system of NAEYC's National Academy of Early Childhood Programs is just one example. The time is ripe to devote some of that same energy to devise a rational, integrated lattice of professional development opportunities that begin to function when someone's eyes first light up about pursuing a career in early childhood.

A vision for the profession

Any workable system to articulate professional development in early childhood education should include these principles.

- **Child development knowledge is fundamental.** Good practice based on young children's growth and development is universal, regardless of setting or program auspices.
- **Language skills are a basic tool of good practice.** Teacher language proficiency—in English and families' home languages—enriches the educational experiences of children, facilitates parent education and advocacy efforts, and makes the award of academic credit meaningful.
- **Professional growth opportunities should be offered at two levels of participation.** One level would enhance practical "how-to" skills; the other would require discussion, reflection, and literate student responses that merit academic credit.
- **Standards of quality should be set for professional development at all levels, under all auspices.** Course content, duration, and credentials and experience of instructors would meet recognized standards.
- **Traditional assumptions must be examined and changed.** Articulation between CDA preparation, two-year, and four- or five-year programs must be achieved, with some compromise expected by all parties. The majority of children in the United States are involved in some type of early childhood education, so demand for professionals is certain. Training institutions, government agencies, and politicians will all have their best interests met when they work together to ensure that young children are served effectively and efficiently. Streamlining training and establishing incentives for professional development are the places to begin.
- **Barriers to instruction must be overcome.** The excuse that attending school is a hardship must no longer be valid. There are a myriad of

> *Segmenting care and education is not only pointless and divisive, but developmentally inappropriate!*

ways to offer academic credit—weekend seminars, Saturday classes, bilingual instruction, television classes, cassette courses, and on-site instruction—that reduce barriers for low-income, single-parent, and employed students.

- **Agencies must work together.** Head Start and state social service and education agencies must acknowledge the similarities of their programs. Segmenting care and education is not only pointless and divisive, but developmentally inappropriate! Cross-agency standards for early childhood staff functions, competencies, and levels of education must be designed. When agencies cooperate, choice will be preserved, but the chaos will be eliminated.

- **Standards must be common knowledge.** An all-out media blitz would penetrate the American consciousness. Students would know which courses and experiences, including teacher certification, would advance them toward their goals. Families would know the level of expertise to demand for their children. The general public would be informed about and recognize the justice of comparable compensation for practitioners with comparable credentials performing comparable work in all settings. Stability of staff, and improved program quality, would be the result.

Articulated, standardized professional development systems and criteria would eliminate the nightmare from the dream of working with young children and enable all early childhood practitioners to serve children and their parents better.

A New Century/A New System for Professional Development

Gwen Morgan

State policies greatly affect career development in early childhood education, as Jones, Whitehead, and Hutchison (in this volume) note. An analysis of these policies by The Center for Career Development in Early Care and Education (Morgan et al., 1993; see Part IV in this volume) led to these conclusions:

- The required training and qualifications, established as public policy by child care licensing, are inadequate.
- State requirements for early childhood teacher certificates are not good enough.
- The higher education system for early childhood education is fragmented and inconsistent.
- Availability of informal training is haphazard.
- Public commitment to financing early childhood career preparation is weak and undependable.

These systemic problems reveal that professional preparation in early childhood functions much like a leaky funnel (Figure 1). Most individuals enter the field in roles that require little or no professional preparation. Many eventually complete certificate and degree programs and advance their careers by taking on greater and more varied responsibilities. But not all. Low salaries and the lack of perceived potential for career advancement cause many practitioners to drop out, or leak out of the funnel, before they pursue a CDA or enroll in a college certificate or degree program. If colleges reduced barriers to preparation programs, and if the profession's reward systems were more clearly tied to increased training, the number of individuals seeking further growth, and staying in the funnel, would be much greater.

Early childhood: a leaky funnel

The funnel also illustrates the multiple and progressive levels of professional preparation in the field. Training can be entered at any point. People with more knowledge and skills should be able to enter more responsible and better-paying roles.

In the quest for professionalism, the following primary concerns must be reconciled. Undoubtedly, some trade-offs must be made among these concerns or some may need to be abandoned.

Facing competing concerns

- **Low child-staff ratios.** Ratios affect quality; they also drive cost.
- **Available labor pool.** Programs for young children are labor intensive. A large but feasible labor pool is needed to staff these positions.
- **Many forms of care.** Center programs, family child care, and many other diverse types of early childhood education are offered.

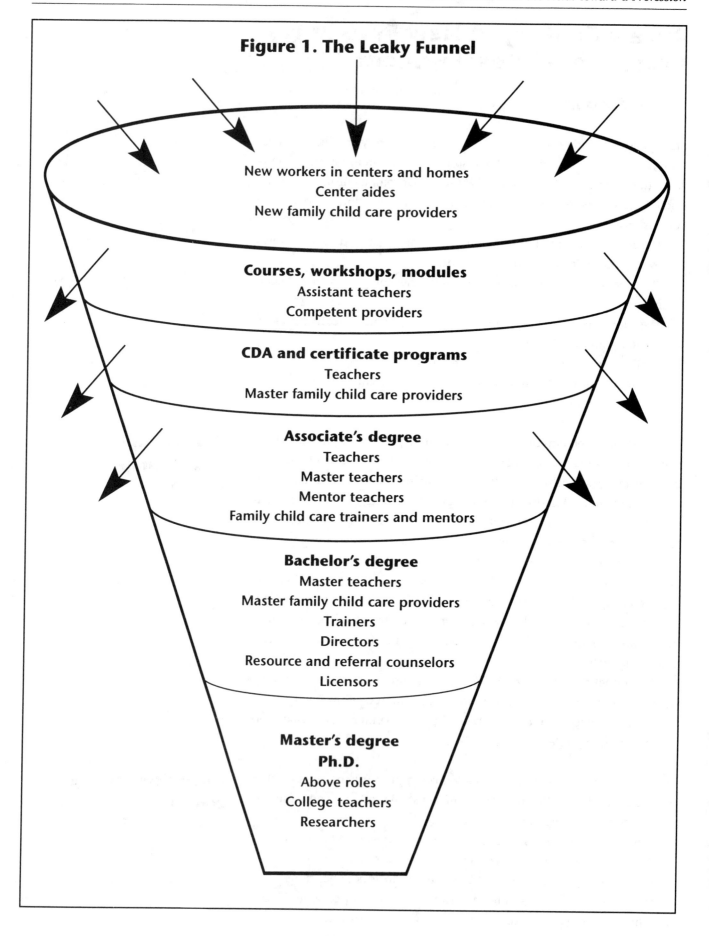

Figure 1. The Leaky Funnel

New workers in centers and homes
Center aides
New family child care providers

Courses, workshops, modules
Assistant teachers
Competent providers

CDA and certificate programs
Teachers
Master family child care providers

Associate's degree
Teachers
Master teachers
Mentor teachers
Family child care trainers and mentors

Bachelor's degree
Master teachers
Master family child care providers
Trainers
Directors
Resource and referral counselors
Licensors

Master's degree
Ph.D.
Above roles
College teachers
Researchers

- **Improved compensation.** Inadequate compensation increases turnover and erodes quality.
- **A mix of staff that includes college graduates.** Higher quality is more likely when teachers with a sufficient depth of professional preparation serve as role models.
- **Focus on the whole child.** Education and care are inseparable.
- **Developmentally appropriate programming.** Depth of training in specialty areas such as infants, toddlers, school-age children, and children with special needs is not equivalent to elementary education knowledge and skills.
- **Qualifications that vary by roles and levels within roles.** The field offers a variety of professional roles, including but not limited to classroom teacher.
- **Access to employment and advancement regardless of ethnicity, race, or income.** Employment opportunities in respected roles for parents and community members are an integral and necessary part of good programs for young children.
- **Partnership with parents.** A shared working relationship with parents reflects the knowledge base of the profession and must be included in any model of professional development.
- **Professional recognition.** The profession has yet to clearly define the goal it seeks.

Low salaries and the lack of perceived potential for career advancement cause many practitioners to drop out, or leak out of the funnel, before they pursue a CDA or enroll in a college certificate or degree program.

These concerns may seem like givens. They are not. Some of these factors compete with each other. Within the field, there are some who are ready to exchange one or more of these concerns, if necessary, to achieve the goal of professionalism. Others are ready to sacrifice everything to retain these same items. A closer look at each is in order.

The profession is not in total agreement on low child-staff ratios. Some experts point out that other countries, such as France, do not have the ratios recommended here. This concern plays directly into the trilemma of wages, affordability, and ratios.

What about the feasibility of the labor pool? Many in the field believe programs should be staffed solely with college graduates. Given the need for low staff-child ratios, sheer economics would make such a goal impossible. The result would be limited availability of child care, rather than a pouring of labor into the field.

Surely there is unanimity on maintaining diversity of forms of care? Again, there are those in the field who sincerely feel that experts know more than parents about the best forms of child care. Some may believe that center care is so obviously superior that family child care should be eliminated. Equally firmly, some assert that family child care is so superior that centers should be eliminated, especially for infants. Many policymakers appear to believe that care by relatives, unlicensed family child care, and in-home care are superior to either centers or family child care. Others will abandon these forms of care altogether.

Trading off any of these cherished values may not be necessary along the route to professional recognition and/ or better compensation and quality care for children.

Does everyone agree on improved compensation? This issue is not as clear as it first appears, because of clashing views on trade-offs among compensation, affordability, and ratios. Improved compensation is an absolute goal for some, while others want to imbed that pursuit in an effort to address the trilemma of wages, fees, and ratios. Distrust and miscommunication are pitfalls to collaboration on this and some other issues.

Is a mix of staff a common goal for centers? As already pointed out, some would settle for nothing short of all staff having college degrees. Others would settle for the CDA Credential for all. The idea that good centers would be staffed by some with degrees, some with CDAs, and others in training is not frequently expressed as a goal.

Most people in the profession believe there is consensus on the concept of care and education as inseparable for young children, especially the very youngest children. This whole-child focus leads to criticism of the idea that a system would employ a "teacher" in the morning and "caregivers" in the afternoon. Yet there are those who would trade part of the whole-child concept to get higher pay for teachers.

NAEYC has been a strong leader in educating other disciplines and the public about developmentally appropriate practice. But how many colleges trade off depth of knowledge in infant programming in order to provide an elementary teaching credential along with the early childhood degree?

The child care system offers a variety of roles with varying qualifications of experience and education. Many believe in a system that emphasizes lifelong personal growth and dynamic reward systems. Yet many others focus only on the role of classroom teacher and view that role in a very static way.

An example of failure to build in professional development incentives is found in recently adopted regulations for group child care home providers in one eastern state. Group home providers, aided by an employed assistant, are allowed to serve up to 12 children. Providers are required to complete an entry-level training course in order to get a three-year license. At the end of their third year, the state requires providers to repeat the entry-level training to be re-licensed. What kind of insanity leads to writing a requirement like that?

Another issue with clashing trade-offs is director qualifications. Research indicates that the quality of a center depends on the director, and that directors should have all the knowledge and skills of the master teacher level plus other leadership and administrative skills to create a healthy, supportive organization for teachers, parents, and children. Good former teachers often make the best directors. But some in the field resist requiring and providing additional administrative training because of a fear of undermining the role of the teacher, which they see as the sole professional role.

How committed is the profession to diversity in employment access? Pride is often expressed that we have a few parent aides who eventually pursue higher education and earn advanced degrees. We know that children need role models of success from their own culture and community. However, some would trade this goal for more professional recognition.

Early childhood education as a profession appears to have a greater commitment to partnership with parents than most related fields. Although this commitment may not be traded off, few are trained to know and feel what it means in depth. Some cling to the attitude that a professional knows more than parents about what is best for their children.

Finally, how widespread is the yearning for professionalism and professional recognition? The goal is frequently expressed by family child care providers and center staff, but it is by no means a universal goal. Many would trade professionalism for one or more of these other concerns. Of those who embrace professionalism, there are major differences in how it is viewed and defined.

Trading off any of these cherished values may not be necessary along the route to professional recognition and/or better compensation and quality care for children. As the 21st century approaches, outmoded 19th-century assumptions can be discarded in favor of a new vision for the profession.

One key need for a contemporary model is a dynamic perception of a variety of professional roles and the development of qualifications and reward systems that are progressive. A static view of professional development leads to seeing only the role of teacher—and there is no agreement on what is appropriate and feasible preparation for that role. Some believe that a baccalaureate or higher degree is necessary; others would set the basic requirement at the associate degree level. Still others pursue the goal of CDA credentialing as sufficient, and there are those who argue for specially designed courses or local certificates.

A dynamic model of professionalism

The child care system offers a variety of roles with varying qualifications of experience and education.

Before a dynamic model of career development can fully evolve, the barriers in current training systems must be removed. Two "brick walls" were described earlier by Hutchison (this volume): the wall between training in non-college systems and certificate and degree programs and the wall between associate and baccalaureate degree institutions.

In an effort to conceptualize these two different training systems, and to visualize a bridge between them, The Center for Career Development in Early Care and Education devised a career progression model (Figure 2).

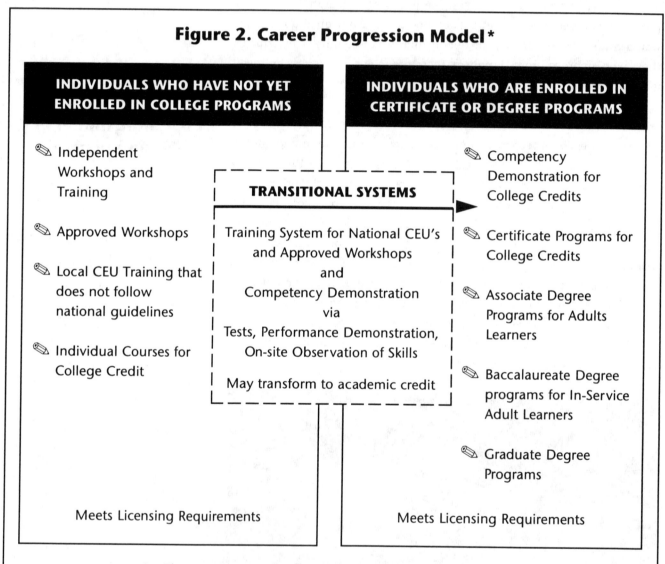

Figure 2. Career Progression Model*

| **INDIVIDUALS WHO HAVE NOT YET ENROLLED IN COLLEGE PROGRAMS** | **INDIVIDUALS WHO ARE ENROLLED IN CERTIFICATE OR DEGREE PROGRAMS** |

- Independent Workshops and Training
- Approved Workshops
- Local CEU Training that does not follow national guidelines
- Individual Courses for College Credit

TRANSITIONAL SYSTEMS

Training System for National CEU's and Approved Workshops
and
Competency Demonstration
via
Tests, Performance Demonstration, On-site Observation of Skills

May transform to academic credit

- Competency Demonstration for College Credits
- Certificate Programs for College Credits
- Associate Degree Programs for Adults Learners
- Baccalaureate Degree programs for In-Service Adult Learners
- Graduate Degree Programs

Meets Licensing Requirements   Meets Licensing Requirements

*   The two systems are "bridged by the Transitional System.
Units in all the Systems are fully articulated with one another.

Amended by Gwen Morgan and Joan Costley from *Delaware First . . . Again. The First Comprehensive State Training Plan for Child Care Staff* (Brown, N., Costley, J., & Morgan, G.). Final Report of Planning Project, May 1990, p. 26.

The system on the left, which could be loosely called the pre-college system, consists of various preservice and in-service courses and training that meet state child care licensing requirements (courses, credit, clock hours). The system on the right represents degree and certificate programs. People in the field who enter in the pre-college system may at some point enroll in this second system of college programs. The bridging box between the two systems represents an action plan for an overall career development system.

Most state policies and funding are directed toward one or the other of these two systems, thus strengthening the brick walls. The first national policy effort to encourage a single system from pre-college training through higher education was included in provisions of the 1992 Higher Education Act. Issues of transformation to credit and issues of articulation will be important challenges to our profession.

Opportunity for change

Every state has the opportunity to develop additional, and more dynamic, training through the Child Care and Development Block Grant. Doing so will require patience and tolerance to listen to each other's concerns.

A dynamic perspective envisions both lateral and circular professional progression with the same role as well as from role to role. A person may leave and later return to direct service work, possibly in a more specialized role. Direct service may be with parents or with children. Regardless of whether the role is "teacher" or something else, specialists will always continue to rely on their professional knowledge and skills as they move into the rich array of positions in the field.

Without a foundation of professional knowledge, licensors will not be able to regulate helpfully; directors will not know how to maintain policy or support staff; and parent counselors at resource and referral agencies will not have knowledge to share with parents. From the dynamic perspective, the whole field benefits when those not currently working directly with children are familiar with the knowledge base of the profession. For those who continue to work directly with children, salaries should increase when additional knowledge and skills are gained.

This dynamic model of professional preparation has been evolving for many years, and some pieces of it are in place. Many centers, for example, have personnel policies that include a salary scale that rewards staff for higher levels of training and continued work experience. Some state child care licensing requirements have two levels of teacher qualifications, and some have two or more levels for director qualifications as well. A few training programs span from basic entry-level training to degree programs, preparing people for continued career opportunities rather than dead-end roles. Many colleges offer accessible training to those already employed in the field. Some states are developing comprehensive early childhood training plans to incorporate career development possibilities. Some compensation strategies, such as mentor teacher, are tied to role.

A dynamic perspective envisions both lateral and circular professional progression with the same role as well as from role to role.

These emerging practices, all of which reflect a dynamic perspective, may indicate a trend toward a more enlightened vision of professional development. A dynamic system holds the promise for these and many other advantages.

- Full realization of early childhood professional goals without dropping the ideal that members of a child's community, who may not have had access to college, be employed in respected roles in programs.

- Improved quality of care through more coherent identification of both the content of professional training and the level at which it needs to be taught.

- Realistic recognition that low child-staff ratios require many more staff than elementary or secondary education, and that drawing on a college- and a non-college-trained labor force will provide this important pool.

- Potential for higher salaries related to retention and increased qualifications so that salary equity keyed to qualifications can be developed across the different systems that offer programs for young children, such as public schools, Head Start, and communities.

- Opportunity for professional salaries for all staff willing to pursue professional development, rather than settling for a two-class staffing system analogous to military officers and enlisted personnel.

References

Brown, N., Costley, J., & Morgan, G. (1990). *Delaware first . . . again. The first comprehensive state training plan for child care staff.* Boston, MA: The Center for Career Development in Early Care and Education.

Morgan, G., Azer, S., Costley, J., Genser, A., Goodman, I., Lombardi, J., & McGimsey, B. (1993). *Making a career of it: The state of the states report on career development in early care and education.* Boston, MA: The Center for Career Development in Early Care and Education.

Envision the Day: Developing Professional Standards

Jan McCarthy

Good programs for children rely on competent staff—this belief is supported by research and has remained constant over time. High-quality professional preparation programs are central to the development of a competent early childhood staff. We also know that the challenges facing educators of young children have never been greater. For example:

- Populations of children in the United States have become much more diverse, while the teaching force has become less diverse.
- A larger number of children with special needs are being served.
- The increasingly competitive and technologically advanced educational environment necessitates greater expertise of graduates.
- Demand for early childhood programs is high.

This last challenge, the care and education of our youngest and most vulnerable citizens, creates a dilemma for the field. Should early childhood programs retain the present two-tiered system and operate as if the early years have no significant impact on later school and life experiences? With the notable exception of some Head Start programs, developmentally appropriate services with competent teachers are available primarily for those who can afford the high cost. Services of lesser quality typically serve low-income populations of children, who probably have the most to gain from a high-quality experience.

Each of these challenges calls for an investment in the future. This investment is greatly influenced by the way policymakers think about early childhood education and professional development.

The Education of American Teachers focused on the need to restructure

Good programs for children rely on competent staff.

teacher education (Conant, 1963). During the 30 years since that study was released, a great deal of "teacher bashing" has taken place, some of which may be justified, much of which is not. A number of committees and commissions thoughtfully assessed the full range of education issues and proposed directions in publications such as *A Nation At Risk* (National Commission on Excellence in Education, 1983), *The National Education Goals Report* (National Education Goals Panel, 1991), and *Beyond Rhetoric: A New Agenda for Children and Families* (National Commission on Children, 1991). From this turmoil, a climate was created that is much more receptive to reform, a climate with significant implications for early childhood professional development.

State of the profession

An analysis of certification of early childhood teachers in the 50 states and the District of Columbia revealed a broad range of patterns (McCarthy, 1988). Regulations have changed little since the survey was completed (Morgan et al., 1993). Some states have no standards to prepare teachers to work with children younger than elementary school age. A few states have well-defined preparation programs. Others offer certification (licensure) with no specified professional study or preservice experience with young children. Even more discouraging, some state officials indicated during the McCarthy study's interview process that there was no need for professional preparation standards for teachers of young children.

Why is teacher licensure a concern when many programs serving young children fall outside the regulatory domain of state departments of education? Regardless of the type of setting, children's early experiences influence their development. The field of early childhood education must be recognized as an integral part of the educational process that begins at birth and continues throughout life—not as a holding place until children start "real" school. Early childhood educators are far more apt to provide developmentally appropriate experiences for children and to engage in supportive interactions with parents when they have successfully completed a focused program of professional preparation that is rooted in the principles of child growth and development. Understanding and nurturing development is a complex process.

The lack of consistent teacher licensure standards weakens our field in at least three ways:

1. Lack of standards hinders the development of comprehensive preparation programs. States determine teacher licensure standards, and these standards tend to drive the course offerings at institutions of higher education. Justification of expenditures for developing a comprehensive, high-quality teacher preparation program (which goes beyond the feeble standards required by many states) is essential. Early childhood faculty members tend to lack the leverage necessary to convince those who control program development and allocate resources.

2. Lack of standards diminishes the perceived significance of young

children and their needs. Without a stated knowledge base and expected standards of professional performance, teachers of young children will continue to hover at the low end of the salary continuum and will only exercise meager voices in the policymaking arena. Experiences during the early years of children's lives will continue to be viewed as important only if resources are available after other program needs are met. Do we really believe that teaching young children is of lesser value than teaching elementary school, art, or mathematics?

3. Lack of standards perpetuates an uneven system of professional preparation. Due to tremendous variation in state standards, an unevenness of professional knowledge exists across the country. Don't **all** young children have the right to a competent teacher, or will some be denied that privilege because of where they live?

If *early childhood* education is to be accepted as a profession, it must be viewed within the context of teacher education. The following perspectives shed light on NAEYC's relationship with the National Council for Accreditation of Teacher Education (NCATE) and their collaborative efforts to support the goal of early childhood professionalism.

Arthur Wise, President of NCATE, points out that teacher education has failed thus far to implement the mechanisms other fields use to guide and control quality. Teaching and teacher education have an irregular reputation, in part, because schools/colleges of education, unlike schools serving other professions, have not been held to rigorous national standards. Not all educators agree that everyone loses when institutions refuse to submit professional schools to external evaluation by peers. Losses are inevitable, however, when the profession cannot fully command the respect of those outside the field and subject itself to regulation. Virtually every profession, with the exception of teaching, licenses professionals only after they have graduated from an accredited program. These professions expend time, money, and effort to ensure the accreditation of their programs. State governments carefully monitor who can use the title *lawyer, architect,* or *nurse.*

Educators are not as discriminating. Every year, many public schools open with an array of teachers. Some have no formal preparation in their teaching area, but are allowed to practice with a temporary permit; others are graduates from accredited programs. Unlike other professions, novices typically are given the toughest jobs, often without support or supervision. The assignment of unqualified teachers—especially to work with children who are at risk of school or social failure—is scandalous. Across the country, the vast majority of the unqualified teach in large metropolitan areas, where schools scramble to find teachers. In these schools, the least-qualified teachers are always assigned to the students who most need what teachers have to offer. In some districts, a student may, in every year of school, be taught by someone who is uncertified, unqualified, or at best a first-year teacher.

Early childhood teacher education clearly is part of a system with some

Virtually every profession, with the exception of teaching, licenses professionals only after they have graduated from an accredited program.

The coalition of 28 professional organizations that make up NCATE, one of which is NAEYC, are working together to positively influence all teacher education.

flaws. However, the coalition of 28 professional organizations that make up NCATE, one of which is NAEYC, are working together to positively influence all teacher education. Their work holds special meaning for NAEYC and the profession.

One such NCATE process is to increase the number of states with which it collaborates. The major purposes of these efforts are to improve the review process by reducing duplication of effort, to develop a common core of expectations for teacher education, and to develop a state-of-the-art accreditation system compatible with outcome-based state licensing and national certification. As of April 1994, 33 states coordinate their review procedures with NCATE (see Table 2). An additional 10 states are working to meet eligibility criteria for a partnership agreement.

Most of these agreements are developed when deans of colleges of education and directors of teacher education urge their state departments of education to coordinate with NCATE. Partnerships between NCATE and state agencies may be individually negotiated to accommodate one of the three following frameworks:

1. NCATE unit standards and NCATE-approved curriculum guidelines

2. NCATE unit standards and NCATE-approved state program standards

3. NCATE unit standards and an outcome-based state licensing system that uses NCATE-approved specialty organization guidelines in its design

Under option 1 listed above, institutions prepare folios describing how their programs comply with NCATE-approved curriculum guidelines of specialty organizations affiliated with NCATE. As such an organization, NAEYC reviews the early childhood program folios to determine if the program complies with NAEYC's guidelines for early childhood teacher education.

Table 2. State/NCATE Partnerships

Alabama	Montana
Arkansas	Nevada
California	New Mexico
Florida	North Carolina
Georgia	North Dakota
Hawaii	Ohio
Idaho	Oklahoma
Illinois	Oregon
Indiana	Pennsylvania
Iowa	South Dakota
Kansas	Tennessee
Kentucky	Virginia
Maine	Washington
Maryland	West Virginia
Massachusetts	Wisconsin
Michigan	Wyoming
Mississippi	

Under option 2, NAEYC reviews the state's standards for program approval in relation to NAEYC guidelines. The first two options, implemented with NCATE flexibility, characterize all 33 partnerships. For example, a triad relationship in Florida includes program reviews required by the Board of Regents, which monitors all programs in state universities.

The third NCATE option was adopted in October 1992 and has the potential to link professional accreditation to state licensure in a new way to help ensure well-prepared and competent teachers. In this partnership model, states implement outcome-based licensing systems that assess teachers' knowledge and skills. The Council of Chief State School Officers, a number of states, NCATE, and other stakeholders participate in the Interstate New Teacher Assessment and Support Consortium (INTASC, 1992) which developed the *Model Standards for Beginning Teacher Licensing and Development*. The ten INTAC standards are included in NCATE's refined standards that link licensure and accreditation.

Participants in this third form of NCATE/state partnership are expected to have licensure systems that meet professional teaching standards established by specialty organizations such as NAEYC. As these licensure systems are implemented, they will direct assessments of the effectiveness of programs that prepare new teacher graduates. This information will be taken into account as future accreditation and program approval decisions are made.

Under the agreement, institutions will not be required to complete folios, because the state licensing system will be constructed using national professional association standards. A few states will serve as pilot test sites for the new partnership agreement. This approach will simultaneously strengthen licensing (state certification) and accreditation while simplifying the process and eliminating unnecessary duplication, regulation, and paperwork.

NCATE's Task Force on Performance-Based Licensing and Professional Accreditation, composed of members from the four major stakeholder groups involved in teacher education accreditation—practitioners, teacher educators, specialists, and policymakers—first met in March 1993. The Task Force developed criteria that define the kind of information that states must address in this new system in order to work with NCATE to implement the new model. Because this is a pioneering effort that calls for evidence of what teachers should be able to do as well as what teachers should know, the process is one that will evolve through work with the first states that move to this new system. Currently, Kentucky is working toward developing an outcome-based licensure system and collaborating with the Task Force to develop the new partnership model for accreditation. Through the experiences with Kentucky the criteria and procedures will be revised and refined.

As they work together, NCATE and the states will establish linkages between preservice programs and licensure requirements. Most states cer-

Ultimately, the profession can develop an integrated system in which accreditation of programs, state licensure, and advanced certification standards will complement and reinforce one another.

tify individuals based on courses taken. Now, outcome-oriented standards can be developed by the national professional association in conjunction with states. These standards can be used to design assessments of teacher knowledge and performance, creating new connections between preservice education standards and initial performance, or licensing standards. Ultimately, the profession can develop an integrated system in which accreditation of programs, state licensure, and advanced certification standards, such as those being developed by the National Board of Professional Teaching Standards, will complement and reinforce one another.

The paradigm shift

Moving to outcome-oriented standards calls for a serious paradigm shift that focuses on a description of critical teacher performances that are demonstrated through *authentic* teaching tasks: tasks teachers are expected to experience and address in the workplace. The distinguishing difference between outcome-based programs and the competency-based programs of a few years ago is that the latter called for hundreds of competencies demonstrated in isolation, often without experience with children. Features of the paradigm shift are contrasted in Table 3.

Implications for early childhood education

Three significant implications support NAEYC's positions related to teacher education and developmentally appropriate practices for children.

1. Congruence between developmentally appropriate practices for children and preparation of teachers. Congruence between the profession's commitment to developmentally appropriate practices for children and its early childhood teacher preparation programs is essential. *Authentic* teaching tasks defined in outcome-based programs offer this potential, and congruence is increasingly being achieved. The National Council of Teachers of Mathematics developed new standards for student achievement and revised its guidelines for teachers. Forty states are retraining teachers using the new standards.

2. Changes in specialty organizations, guidelines, and folio review process. Specialty organizations—including NAEYC—are revising their national guidelines to focus on outcomes. These guidelines can then be used to create state-of-the-art professional development programs. In the future, these guidelines will be used to create state licensing systems. As a result, specialty organization guidelines will dramatically increase in importance. NAEYC will be in a position to have a much broader influence on how teachers of young children are prepared. When states develop licensing systems that are approved by NAEYC, all institutions in the state will comply with the standards, not just those that choose to submit a folio to NAEYC to review.

3. The unevenness from state to state in preparation of teachers of young children. As states use NAEYC's guidelines to develop licensure standards, young children (regardless of where they live) will have access to teachers who demonstrate professional knowledge and performance. Furthermore, reciprocity between states will enable teachers to move to regions where the job demands are greater or where life circumstances take them, with reasonable assurance that they will be authorized to practice their profession.

Early childhood education must have a vision of its goals for programs serving young children. Envision the day when **every young child** is taught by a knowledgeable, qualified teacher, when **all teachers** of young children engage in practices that result in the development of children who

Table 3. Features of the Paradigm Shift from Competency-Based to Outcome-Based Programs

From primarily inputs	To primarily outcomes
• Acquisition of knowledge and skills (decontextualized)	• Demonstration of application of knowledge and skills in authentic situations
• Demonstration of discrete competencies	• Demonstration of quality performance on integrated tasks (use of knowledge, skills, and judgment)
• Focus on common inputs (courses, clock hours, defined experiences)	• Focus on common outcomes (performance in authentic teaching situations)
• Learning and assessment as separate processes	• Use of performance tasks for learning and assessment
• Coverage of an ever-expanding body of professional knowledge	• Focus on key concepts and processes most critical to students' learning
• Criteria for performance often ill-defined and subject to the supervisor or assessor	• Criteria for performance, defined, made public, and supported by examples
• Teachers/professors as transmitters of knowledge	• Teachers/professors as facilitators of the teaching/learning process and professional growth
• Graduation as the termination of formal learning	• Graduation as a defined level of performance on a continuum, e.g., the path from novice to expert
• Lack of congruence between N–12 learning goals and teacher education or congruent emphasis	• Goals of teacher education and N–12 learning goals congruent in emphasis on performance

From: T. Bliss and R. Pankratz. (1992). Paper presented at the annual conference of the American Association of Colleges of Teacher Education, Atlanta, Georgia.

*Preparation of personnel in a sound professional development system relies heavily on involvement of competent professionals who demonstrate knowledge **and** performance abilities.*

are curious, have a passion for learning, are exuberant about what they can do, and are ready to face challenges.

Envision the day when teachers are held accountable for responsible professional practice and are expected to apply developmentally appropriate practices in an ethical manner; when the early childhood profession attracts a fair share of the best and brightest of both genders and all races who commit to an educational career. Teaching young children will be among the most respectable lines of work. Parents will be pleased when their offspring choose to become, or marry, teachers of young children.

Envision the day when teachers are adequately compensated according to the dictates of the marketplace, when salaries rise to the levels necessary to attract a sufficient high-quality supply of teachers. Salaries will not be artificially depressed as they are now.

To welcome such a day, we must collaborate to ensure that the goals for professionalism are achieved. Commitment to a career lattice requires recognition of the support that is essential for the lattice to work. Preparation of personnel in a sound professional development system relies heavily on involvement of competent professionals who demonstrate knowledge **and** performance abilities.

Is the profession ready and willing to move to outcome-based baccalaureate programs that lead to licensure in order for our system to become a continuous process that encourages upward mobility? If the early childhood teaching profession is to become recognized as a viable profession, it must do what it has never done—create consensus about its goals and then commit collective energy to make them happen.

References

Conant, J.B. (1963). *The education of American teachers.* New York: McGraw Hill.

The Interstate New Teacher Assessment and Support Consortium (INTASC). (1992). *The model standards for beginning teacher licensing and development.* Washington, DC: Council of Chief State School Officers.

McCarthy, J. (1988). *State certification of early childhood teachers.* Washington, DC: NAEYC.

Morgan, G., Azer, S., Costley, J., Genser, A., Goodman, I., Lombardi, J., & McGimsey, B. (1993). *Making a career of it: The state of the states report on career development in early care and education.* Boston, MA: The Center for Career Development in Early Care and Education.

National Commission on Children. (1991). *Beyond rhetoric: A new agenda for children and families.* Washington, DC: Author.

National Education Goals Panel. (1991). *The national education goals report.* Washington, DC: Author.

Part II

Core Content for Professional Development

What content should all early childhood education professionals know and be able to apply in their work with young children and their families? Contributors to Part II scrutinize the many facets of the professional knowledge base that pave the diverse routes toward the field's career lattice. In the process of identifying the basic elements, they underscore the need for specialized professional development options that build on the core knowledge and improve professional practice in specific roles and settings.

The discussion opens with five brief descriptions of various components of the profession's core knowledge. **Carol Brunson Phillips**, Executive Director of the Council for Early Childhood Professional Recognition, examines themes inherent in the Child Development Associate (CDA) Professional Preparation Program that are the basis of knowledge for every early childhood professional.

As a member of the National Association for Bilingual Education and NAEYC's Latino Caucus, **Cecelia Alvarado Kuster** urges the field to recognize the importance of incorporating children's home languages in educational settings. Kuster focuses on five salient competencies for preparing staff to work with culturally and linguistically diverse children and families.

Kay Hollestelle, a former family child care provider, former administrator of NAFCC's accreditation system, and current executive director of The Children's Foundation, describes the role that family child care accreditation plays in articulating and extending the core for family child care providers to establish a comprehensive career lattice. She acknowledges that the profession's knowledge base applies to family child care but extends it to include entrepreneurial skills of small business operators and poses questions yet to be resolved.

Barbara J. Smith is executive director of the Division for Early Childhood (DEC) of the Council for Exceptional Children. DEC's 7,000 members are dedicated to promoting policies and practices to support families and enhance the optimal development of children with special needs, from birth through age 8, and their families. Smith focuses on the need for NAEYC, DEC, and other groups to collaborate to prepare all early childhood professionals to work in inclusive programs.

The National Center for the Early Childhood Work Force, formerly the Child Care Employee Project (CCEP), is a resource and advocacy organization dedicated to improving the quality of child care by upgrading professional compensation, working conditions, and access to training. **Marcy Whitebook**, founding executive director of CCEP, urges that professionals

Contributors to Part II underscore the need for specialized professional development options that build on the core knowledge and improve professional practice in specific roles and settings.

be prepared to act as change agents in order to reshape the conditions needed for effective teaching to take place.

Bernard Spodek, former NAEYC president and professor at the University of Illinois, describes six key components of the framework for baccalaureate early childhood teacher education programs. These components also apply to most two-year programs preparing early childhood practitioners. Spodek sets forth a challenge to strengthen the quality and consistency of the knowledge upon which professional practice is based.

Education or care? A contextual model of early childhood professional development is proposed by **Karen VanderVen**, a professor in the School of Social Work at the University of Pittsburgh. She reviews the nature of knowledge and practice, pinpoints factors that impinge on professionalism, and then sets forth a contextual model for the profession that illuminates a way to resolve the thorny dilemma between education and care. VanderVen's proposal leads directly into the strategies to encourage effective professional development that appear in Part III.

At the Core: What Every Early Childhood Professional Should Know

Carol Brunson Phillips

Core knowledge in early childhood education is extensive and comprehensive and goes beyond common knowledge about young children. These five themes address content that every professional in the field should know.

1. Children develop in context. Nearly everyone knows that children grow; they get bigger and stronger. Professionals also ought to know that children *develop*. Development means that humans share predictable patterns of change. It also means that individuals are influenced by predictable contexts and environments—culture and family—and are, by virtue of personal history, unique and idiosyncratic.

Regardless of the depth and breadth of developmental information professionals choose to learn, or the teaching and learning experiences in which they situate themselves, information and experiences build an understanding about how children develop.

Children develop in context

2. Strategies for working with children are constructed each day. Nearly everyone knows that working with children requires encouraging learning through play and implementing activities. Professionals ought to know that deciding what to do and when to do it are acts of creation, not imitation. These decisions are interactive, based on the *relationship* between who children are, who their parents are, and what the profession endorses as appropriate practice.

Effective practitioners put together two informational halves. One half is a repertoire of activities to do with children. The other half is drawn from observations of children and collaboration with parents. Practice is constructed from both sets of information.

Strategies for working with children are constructed each day

3. Effective practice requires a comprehensive set of skills. Nearly everyone knows a little bit about what children need to do—brush their teeth, exercise, drink juice or milk instead of soda. Professionals ought to know that the care and education of children requires a full range of skills. Skills and information related to children's physical development are not enough. Professionals must also have skills and information about a variety of children's needs. These skills are succinctly described by the six Child Development Associate (CDA) competencies and 13 functional areas (Table 4) (Phillips, 1991a, 1991b).

Effective practice requires a comprehensive set of skills

Table 4. CDA Competency Goals and Functional Areas

I. **To establish and maintain a safe, healthy learning environment**

   1. **Safe:** Candidate provides a safe environment to prevent and reduce injuries.

   2. **Health:** Candidate promotes good health and nutrition and provides an environment that contributes to the prevention of illness.

   3. **Learning environment:** Candidate uses space, relationships, materials, and routines as resources for constructing an interesting, secure, and enjoyable environment that encourages play, exploration, and learning.

II. **To advance physical and intellectual competence**

   4. **Physical:** Candidate provides a variety of equipment, activities, and opportunities to promote the physical development of children.

   5. **Cognitive:** Candidate provides activities and opportunities that encourage curiosity, exploration, and problem solving appropriate to the developmental levels and learning styles of children.

   6. **Communication:** Candidate actively communicates with children and provides opportunities and support for children to understand, acquire, and use, verbal and nonverbal means of communicating thoughts and feelings.

   7. **Creative:** Candidate provides opportunities that stimulate children to play with sound, rhythm, language, materials, space, and ideas in individual ways to express their creative abilities.

III. **To support social and emotional development and provide positive guidance**

   8. **Self:** Candidate provides physical and emotional development and emotional security for each child and helps each child to know, accept, and take pride in himself or herself and to develop a sense of independence.

   9. **Social:** Candidate helps each child feel accepted in the group, helps children learn to communicate and get along with others, and encourages feelings of empathy and mutual respect among children and adults.

   10. **Guidance:** Candidate provides a supportive environment in which children can begin to learn and practice appropriate and acceptable behaviors as individuals and as a group.

IV. **To establish positive and productive relationships with families**

   11. **Families:** Candidate maintains an open, friendly, and cooperative relationship with each child's family, encourages their involvement in the program, and supports the child's relationship with his or her family.

V. **To ensure a well-run, purposeful program responsive to participant needs**

   12. **Program management:** Candidate is a manager who uses all available resources to ensure an effective operation. The candidate is a competent organizer, planner, recordkeeper, communicator, and a cooperative co-worker.

VI. **To maintain a commitment to professionalism**

   13. **Professionalism:** Candidate makes decisions based on knowledge of early childhood theories and practices, promotes quality in child care services, and takes advantage of opportunities to improve competence, both for personal and professional growth and for the benefit of children and families.

(Phillips, 1991a, p. 466)

4. Early childhood professionals know they belong to a profession. Nearly everyone knows for whom they work—"I work for General Motors." "I work for Mrs. Jones." "I work for the Army." "I work for Head Start." But early childhood professionals ought to know that they are members of a larger professional group. Among that group are colleagues who perform different roles within agencies and organizations, who have different levels of preparation, and who have different areas of expertise and specialization. All professionals share concerns about issues, professional performance standards, and visions that are distinct and separate from regulatory requirements and perhaps their employers' views. This profession also obligates professionals to engage in activities that go *beyond* the workplace.

Early childhood professionals know they belong to a profession

5. Even skilled professionals have limitations. Nearly everyone thinks that they know everything there is to know about children. Professionals ought to have a healthy appreciation for what they do not know and cannot do. A group of graduate students about to begin their final field experience were asked, "What frightens you about what you're getting ready to do?" When some replied "nothing," there was reason to worry.

Professionals are aware that special education expertise exists, even when they don't have it. Professionals recognize that effective teachers speak children's home languages even if they don't speak the child's language. Professionals know that racism and bias contribute to the underdevelopment of children and families, even when they don't know how to change such conditions.

In the struggle to define the profession's core content—to circumscribe the breadth and the depth of that content, to designate the levels of preparation and their articulation—these themes should distinguish the knowledge base.

Even skilled professionals have limitations

Phillips, C.B. (Ed.). (1991a). *Essentials for Child Development Associates working with young children*. Washington, DC: Council for Early Childhood Professional Recognition.

Phillips, C.B. (Ed.). (1991b). *Seminar instructor's guide for the CDA Professional Preparation Program*. Washington, DC: Council for Early Childhood Professional Recognition.

References

At the Core: Language and Cultural Competence

Cecelia Alvarado Kuster

A group of five Latinas—Lourdes Diaz Soto, Antonia Lopez, Renee Martinez, Marlene Zepeda, and myself have worked to develop guidelines for working with children and families who speak languages other than English (Soto, 1994). These guidelines include

- qualifications of early childhood educators and teacher educators
- recruiting ethnically and linguistically diverse early childhood practitioners
- development of ethnically and linguistically diverse leadership in the field
- culturally and linguistically appropriate practice

The following competencies stand out as essential core content for all early childhood professionals.

Fluency in the child's home language

VISTA and the Peace Corps require intensive language instruction prior to placement of volunteers so that participants can effectively serve their assigned populations. Business representatives are required to develop lan-

One of the most important competencies for professionals working with children and families is fluency in the families' home languages.

guage competencies to carry out their expert activities. These individuals may use a second language for a few months or a few years, but ability to speak the language of the people with whom they work is vital.

Early childhood education professionals often work with populations who are speakers of languages other than English for an entire career. Certainly, then, one of the most important competencies for professionals working with children and families is fluency in the families' home languages. Effective communication with the client group should be a requirement for professional preparation.

The United States holds a minority opinion in believing that the ability to speak one language is sufficient in this changing world. Hutchison (see this volume) and most people in early childhood education assert that language is the base for children's learning. Yet, the profession continues to put children at risk by requiring them to attempt to form concepts and construct social knowledge in an unfamiliar language. Why are children placed in such a difficult learning situation, when adults would never place themselves there?

Focus on family competence

The second critical professional competency is the ability to perceive and relate to children and families from the perspective of the family's competence. Terms such as *limited English speaking* and *non-English speaking* imply deficits. Why not focus on competencies, such as the ability to speak a language other than English?

Professionals should use expressions that respect and define the capabilities of *all* children and families. The development of a caring and sharing dialogue, rather than a charge to help these populations, demonstrates respect. Another way is to view families' interdependent social systems and relationships as positive strategies for social development and survival, rather than as at odds with the majority culture's value of independence.

Enhance culture

The knowledge and ability to preserve and enhance the best of families' cultures is the third competency essential for all early childhood educators. Dances, food, and folk tales have their place as manifestations of culture; but they are not, in and of themselves, the base of culture. *Culture* is the deep structural rules that children learn while being reared in their families and communities. They absorb messages about the values that support life, group stability, and survival.

Teachers, family child care providers, program directors, and teacher educators must all uphold the goal of cultural preservation, or their efforts will lead them, and the families with whom they work, astray. This goal is impossible to achieve without first exploring and accepting the importance of one's own background and cultural identity. Individuals cannot appreciate and value something about someone else that they do not value in their own experience.

Practica give students of early childhood education the firsthand opportunity to experience children in the process of discovery and to see the impact that discovery has on their growth. In turn, students come to value that child's, and their own, experience.

Encourage social responsibility

Professionals in this field are committed to maintain family bonding and encourage social responsibility within the group. Multiage grouping and cross-age teaching foster group ties. This sense of community is an incredibly important value within Latino and other groups, for very deep and long-standing reasons.

Perhaps the greatest strength of the Latino community is its strong belief in, and the cohesiveness of, family. Dysfunctional families exist in every community, but cultural values are not the cause. If development of healthy families is to be encouraged, society must address economic, educational, and social oppression.

Confront biases

Lastly, examination of personal racial attitudes—and initiation of strategies to develop attitudes and practices free of bias and fear—must be undertaken. One such effort is the Leadership in Diversity Project, led by Louise Derman-Sparks, Phyllis Brady, and myself. The project selected 20 members of the California Association for the Education of Young Children to participate in 15 days of learning experiences on issues of diversity over the course of a year. For two years, these interns conducted diversity workshops in their local communities and became certified as CAEYC diversity trainers.

The project's professional development strategies include a survey of research, models of adult learning, bilingual education methodology, and the construction of adult learning opportunities in different settings. However, the major emphasis is on personal and institutional issues related to racism and other biases. Undergraduate and graduate teacher education courses rarely if ever address these issues. They deserve attention in the preparation of all early childhood professionals.

The child's essential sense of self is at risk when the profession lacks caregivers who speak the child's home language and who fail to understand and value the family's childrearing practices and cultural values. NAEYC's leadership is critical to make certain that this essential sense of self is preserved for, or restored to, all children and families.

Resources

Cummins, J. (1981). The role of primary language development in promoting educational success for language minority students. In California State Department of Education, Office of Bilingual Bicultural Education, *Schooling and language minority students: A theoretical framework* (pp. 3–49). Sacramento: California State Department of Education.

Derman-Sparks, L., & the A.B.C. Task Force. (1989). *Anti-bias curriculum: Tools for empowering young children.* Washington, DC: National Association for the Education of Young Children.

McCracken, J.B. (1993). *Valuing diversity: The primary years.* Washington, DC: NAEYC.

Soto, L.D. with Lopez, A., Kuster, C.A., & Martinez, R. (1994). *The early education of linguistically and culturally diverse children.* Unpublished paper.

Wong Fillmore, L. (1991). When learning a second language means losing the first. *Early Childhood Research Quarterly, 6*(3), 323–346.

At the Core: Entrepreneurial Skills for Family Child Care Providers

Kay Hollestelle

Family child care providers are first and foremost nurturers and caregivers, but they are also entrepreneurs. As operators of small businesses, they are unique in the early childhood profession. The term *family child care* is a perfect description. One family brings other families into its home to offer a safe, stimulating, and nurturing environment for young children.

The National Association for Family Child Care (NAFCC) offers a voluntary accreditation program for providers. The program helps to establish good quality family child care settings by identifying the information providers must know. The system's assessment tool incorporates the competency levels found in the CDA (see Table 4 on p. 58) with an additional emphasis on business practices. The evaluation process involves self-evaluation, two outside observations, and a family survey. Each provider writes a report, using scores from the assessment tool and parent surveys as a basis for discussion.

Much work needs to be done if family child care is to be adequately represented within the career lattice.

This program was launched in June 1988, after a year of development, field testing, revising the assessment instrument, and refining the assessment process. Providers retain their accreditation regardless of where they live and must be reaccredited every three years.

From June 1988 to April 1994, 1,022 providers successfully completed NAFCC's accreditation. Thirty of those who are no longer accredited retired after an average of 20 years in the field, having achieved recognition as professionals and distinction among their peers and in their respective communities. Fifty left child care to resume a previous career path. The remaining providers moved on the career lattice into some other area of the early childhood profession. Morgan's image of the leaky funnel (Figure 1 on p. 40) illustrates that more people with experience in the profession might remain on this lattice if there were a systematic approach to providing educational opportunities.

The profession's knowledge base definitely applies to family child care. However, much work needs to be done if family child care is to be adequately represented within the career lattice. Among the questions still to be answered are these:

1. How does NAFCC's accreditation fit within the goals of the larger profession and a professional development system?

2. How does the training family child care providers receive compare with other levels of knowledge and abilities?

3. How can current delivery systems provide educational opportunities for family child care providers?

Family child care providers are first and foremost nurturers and caregivers.

With attention to these and other issues, the needs of this diverse group can be met within the early childhood education profession. A system of professional development opportunities will be possible because family child care providers are unified in their desire that young children—regardless of child care setting—receive high-quality services.

At the Core: The Special Needs of Children with Disabilities

Barbara J. Smith

A primary goal of The Division for Early Childhood (DEC) of the Council for Exceptional Children is to ensure access to high-quality services for young children with special needs and their families. Children with special needs include those who have disabilities, developmental delays, are gifted and talented, or are at risk of future developmental disabilities. To meet this goal, DEC engages in professional development, public policy, research, and collaboration with parents and other professional organizations.

Federal and state laws have greatly improved access to services for young children with disabilities. The Americans with Disabilities Act (ADA) ensures access to public accommodations and services for people with disabilities. Programs through P.L. 99-457, the Individuals with Disabilities Education Act (IDEA), serve children from birth through age 21. Services for young children are to be provided in the least restrictive environment. States that participate in the federal infant and toddler program under P.L. 99-457 must assure services for all children with disabilities from birth.

Achieving the second aspect of DEC's goal, the high quality of services, is still a challenge. Many critical issues drive the field toward quality, including the need for services to be family-centered and family-driven, and the requirement that services for children with disabilities be provided in mainstream or inclusive environments. Why should children be served in inclusive environments?

Federal and state laws have greatly improved access to services for young children with disabilities, but achieving high-quality services is still a challenge.

1. Children who are served with their typically developing peers develop at least as well or more fully than those served in segregated settings (Strain, 1990; Smith & Rose, 1993). Research shows benefits in growth, particularly in language and social development, for young children with disabilities who receive services in settings with typically developing children.

2. Parents want their children to be placed in inclusive settings. Parents repeatedly express the desire that their young children with disabilities have friends from their neighborhood who are typically developing.

3. The law requires program options that include normalized environments. P.L. 99-457 and the ADA both require that services for children with disabilities be available in the least restrictive environment.

With this movement toward mainstream services, early childhood special educators are rethinking their appropriate roles. Indeed, the field encourages schools and other agencies to give parents the option of having their child's special education and related services delivered in child care, Head Start, pre-kindergarten, and other normalized community settings. **If the goal is to have children served in neighborhood programs, then all early childhood practitioners will work with children with disabilities. Every practitioner will need the skills to meet the diverse abilities of all young children.**

This trend leads to several questions: What are the core skills that every early childhood professional will need to work with children with disabilities? Are there special skills that every practitioner will not need? If so, what are these skills and who should have this specialty? Should specialists be in every program, or serve as resources and consultants?

DEC has identified a set of competencies that reflect the diverse learn-

Children who are served with their typically developing peers develop at least as well or more fully than those served in segregated settings.

ing needs of young exceptional children. We are currently developing a position and concept paper describing the new roles and professional standards applicable to early childhood special educators. Coupled with the position on teacher certification adopted by the Association of Teacher Educators (ATE) and NAEYC (1991), early childhood competencies would address the learning needs of nearly all children. Nevertheless, some very real challenges remain in the area of professional development and credentialing.

* The field would benefit from a clearly defined set of the competencies needed at entry and advanced levels for all early childhood personnel to help them feel supported, eager, and competent to work with children with disabilities and their families.
* A clear vision is needed for the emerging role of the early childhood special educator and other pediatric specialty areas, such as occupational therapy, physical therapy, social work, or speech and language therapy.

The field already shares a commitment to meet these challenges and to ensure that children with a wide range of abilities have access to the highest quality services in the mainstream environment. Enthusiasm and excitement are building about the opportunities ahead, about new efforts to finally bring the entire field together, and to ask, "What are the competencies we need to have? How can we work together to ensure best practices for *all* children?"

NAEYC endorsed a DEC position statement on inclusion of children with disabilities into natural environments.

High-quality, coordinated early childhood services for all children and families depend upon many levels of collaboration. NAEYC endorsed a DEC position statement on inclusion of children with disabilities into natural environments (DEC, 1993). The two groups are collaborating on conference presentations and public policy initiatives. DEC, NAEYC, and ATE are preparing materials related to personnel development and credentialing.

National, state, and local groups must work together on issues including accreditation, credentialing, training, CDA competencies, and policies. Together, professional groups can articulate a vision for early childhood professionals who feel supported and competent to serve the needs of all children and their families.

References

Association of Teacher Educators and the National Association for the Education of Young Children. (1991). Early childhood teacher certification. *Young Children, 47*(1), 16–21.

Division for Early Childhood, Council for Exceptional Children (DEC). (1993). *Position statement on inclusion.* Pittsburgh, PA: Author.

Smith, B.J., & Rose, D.F. (1993). *The administrator's policy handbook on preschool mainstreaming.* Brookline, MA: Brookline Books, Inc.

Strain, P.S. (1990). Least restrictive environment (LRE) for preschool children with handicaps: What we know and what we should be doing. *Journal of Early Intervention, 14*(4), 291–296.

At the Core: Advocacy to Challenge the Status Quo

Marcy Whitebook

In the early 1970s, I taught in an underfunded community-based child care program housed in a church. Eager to pursue professional training, and anxious for guidance about how to manage the many challenges of the job, I entered the local university's early childhood education extension program. This innovative program permitted me to arrange a part-time student teaching experience in the university lab school while continuing to work at my other child care job (an unusual opportunity because most university programs are relatively inflexible).

There was a world of difference between the student teaching and daily work environments. The lab school was rich in staff role models and materials. The community program was ill-equipped with both. At the lab school, there were almost enough wheel toys for each child to have one, while at the child care center, about a dozen children vied for the opportunity to ride one working vehicle. It was almost impossible to translate what I was learning at the university into practice at my job because the basic ingredients were so different. Discouragement and frustration were the result.

Several years later, as an instructor in a university lab school, my frustration reappeared. How could I prepare students for the world of work? Competent student teachers should experience a well-endowed program, but must also be alert to the obstacles they would face in most programs. The lab school had a one-to-five ratio of adults to preschoolers (sometimes more), yet students went on to be hired with sole responsibility for a dozen 3-year-olds. When the first group of graduates returned to visit, they made it clear that the realities of their work environments made it difficult for them to apply what they had worked so hard to master.

These stories are not the exception, but are symptomatic of early childhood education as it faces the 21st century. Lack of well-prepared practitioners is just one part of the problem. Many of our best-trained teachers are not adequately prepared for the challenges they face on the job—the realities of a drastically underfunded service. What are some of the barriers to implementation of developmentally appropriate practices?

- Too little, and often damaged, equipment, and materials.
- Unmanageable adult-child ratios.
- Co-workers with little or no training.
- Extraordinarily high staff turnover which is demoralizing and demanding for those who remain.
- Lack of familiarity with the cultures and sometimes the language of children and families.

Many of our best-trained teachers are not adequately prepared for the challenges they face on the job—the realities of a drastically underfunded service.

- Increasing numbers of children and families living in poverty or facing other stressful conditions such as escalating community violence.
- The practical hardships, the assault to self-esteem, and the erosion of hope for a viable career choice that accompanies working for poverty-level wages, inadequate or non-existent benefits, and with little respect for the skills demanded by the job.

All of these realities undermine the ability of many early childhood educators to be effective. These conditions are a logical outgrowth of this nation's lack of genuine commitment to quality early childhood education opportunities as a basic entitlement for children and families.

Given this situation, the core curriculum for early childhood practitioners must incorporate knowledge and skills to enable them to challenge and reshape the conditions for effective teaching. Professionals must be prepared to be agents of change as well as competent practitioners. Some may argue that the goal of our core curriculum should be limited to preparing effective teachers. If the profession's goal is to ensure the well-being of young children, however, then it is unprofessional to allow the status quo, which is harmful to children, to go unchallenged.

The Anti-Bias Curriculum (Derman-Sparks & the A.B.C. Task Force, 1989) encourages staff to examine the hidden assumptions about race, sex, sexual preference, and class that are embedded in teaching practices. We also must examine these assumptions with respect to our profession and the services we provide. By failing to prepare people to become what Takanishi (1980) calls "articulate practitioners," early childhood educators are far more likely to condone the status quo of inadequate services for children and the untenable livelihood for themselves and their colleagues which reflect class and gender biases.

More than piecemeal efforts are needed to remedy this situation. Just as an anti-bias curriculum for children cannot merely be a series of disconnected activities about different cultural customs, but must be an integral part of the entire curriculum, change agents cannot be created by a few idle exercises such as writing a letter to a lawmaker. Rather, advocacy efforts must be woven through the curriculum for early childhood practitioners.

This is not to suggest that learning about child development theory or developmentally appropriate practice be abandoned. In addition to the core knowledge of the profession, practitioners must be armed with the weapons to enforce these theories and implement treasured practices. These are strong words, but reality requires a bold response. Understandings of these topics must be addressed during the course of an integrated professional development experience:

- Why early childhood professional identity involves working for change, and the development of critical thinking skills to evaluate the child care delivery system.

Professionals must be prepared to be agents of change as well as competent practitioners.

In addition to the core knowledge of the profession, practitioners must be armed with the weapons to enforce these theories and implement treasured practices.

- The regulations that govern child care work environments, and knowledge of remedies if violations are encountered.
- Why and how practitioners have and must continue to join together to address the problems facing their profession.

Many students are already being prepared to be change agents as well as competent teachers. During the Worthy Wage Campaign, many college instructors dedicated class time to introduce students to the staffing crisis in the field. Students were encouraged to become involved in this exciting new effort to address the crisis. College campuses have been among the most active sites in carrying out the campaign during its first three years. Many young teachers are committed to making early childhood teaching a career they can afford to pursue.

Preparing early childhood professionals to be change agents will be a departure from standard practice for many. However, it is the only alternative if the work of caring for children is to be valued in our society and if children are to experience the quality of care and education they deserve.

Resources

The National Center for the Early Childhood Work Force, formerly the Child Care Employee Project, is a policy, advocacy, and research organization dedicated to enhancing the compensation, working conditions, and training of child care teachers and family child care providers. The Center also acts as national coordinator of the Worthy Wage Coalition, a grassroots mobilization of caregivers, parents, and others working to confront and reverse the child care staffing crisis. The Coalition sponsors the Worthy Wage Campaign, the focal point of which is a nationwide Worthy Wage Day, held annually during the Week of the Young Child. The National Center also publishes a curriculum, *Working for Quality Child Care*, designed to help students and child care staff become effective advocates for improving quality, salaries, and working conditions in child care programs.

References

Derman-Sparks, L. & the A.B.C. Task Force. (1989). *Anti-bias curriculum: Tools for empowering young children.* Washington, DC: National Association for the Education of Young Children.

Takanishi, R. (1980). *The unknown teacher: Symbolic and structural issues in teacher education.* Keynote speech presented at the Midwest AEYC Conference, Milwaukee, WI.

The Knowledge Base for Baccalaureate Early Childhood Teacher Education Programs

Bernard Spodek

Any description of early childhood teacher preparation programs is complicated by the fact that the field varies geographically. Depending on the state, teacher education programs may prepare teachers to work with children from birth through age 8, or with children from ages 3 to 8, or with children from ages 5 through 8. Some states offer a kindergarten endorsement on an elementary certificate; others have no early childhood certificate at all.

To complicate matters further, qualifications for early childhood teachers vary for different work settings. For example, teachers in public schools are usually prepared in four-year colleges and universities and complete at least a bachelor's degree. Teachers in private preschools and child care centers may be prepared in community or junior colleges and, at most, be required to have a two-year associate degree. Employment in many child care centers may require only rudimentary preparation (Powell & Dunn, 1990).

Teacher education programs are designed to provide students with the knowledge, skills, and attitudes needed to teach young children. These experiences are founded on research, theory, ethical considerations, and practice. Six components of all baccalaureate early childhood teacher education programs, and most two-year programs, are recruitment and selection, general education, professional foundations, instructional knowledge, practice, and program evaluation and modification (Saracho & Spodek, 1983).

Teacher education programs are founded on research, theory, ethical considerations, and practice.

Recruitment and selection

Recruitment of candidates requires actively encouraging people to enter a program; the candidate's selection complements this process by judging applicants for admission. Enrollment procedures in teacher education range from open admissions to rigorous selection.

Teacher education candidates could be judged on personal characteristics. Some suggested characteristics include warmth, enthusiasm, and a businesslike attitude (Ryans, 1960); patience, maturity, energy, encouragement of individual responsibility, and ingenuity in providing teaching and play material (Almy, 1975); flexibility, warmth, and an ability to enjoy and encourage children (Katz, 1969); and the ability to plan and reflect, to tolerate ambiguity, and to make and correct inferences about pupils and teaching techniques (Clark, 1988). Such qualities, to whatever extent they may be related to professional success, are seldom used.

Most four-year teacher preparation institutions use academic achievement, as measured by high school grades and achievement tests, to select students (Lewin & Associates, n.d.). These qualifications remotely relate to teaching success, and entry criteria often vary. When the need for teachers is high, the assessment of teacher candidates is done less carefully and standards are lowered (Applegate, 1987). All programs have some form of a "rolling selection" process, with successful completion of earlier parts of the program required for admission to later parts.

General education

General education is basic to all teacher education programs, but especially to early childhood teacher education programs. It firmly grounds candidates in the culture of the community and the basic structure of scholarly disciplines. Each community's culture must be known if the teacher candidate is to become a part of it and feel comfortable teaching about it. Each discipline provides a unique point of view, style of thinking, and organization of ideas that contribute to teacher preparation.

The content of early childhood education is drawn from general education, including language, social studies, mathematics, science, aesthetics, and humanities. Some content areas are modified to be appropriate to early childhood education. Thus, children's literature, as well as art and music for children, is presented with attention to young children's interests and capacities. Understanding these areas within their parent fields helps give meaning and relevance to the content.

Professional foundations

Professional foundations are concerned with aspects of history, philosophy, sociology, economics, psychology, politics, and anthropology that are the basis for decisions about education. Through foundation courses, teacher candidates learn to restructure their views of children, school, and subjects; analyze American educational patterns in relation to democratic ideals; and have a more humanized vision of the education of society (Gillett & Laska, 1973). These studies can help students become more sensitive to how children from different cultural and economic backgrounds have been treated in school. They can also help students examine and appreciate the aims, ideas, values, influences, and assumptions of a practical education system (Skinner, 1968).

Teachers in early childhood education need to be aware of the history and traditions of their field; of principles of child growth and development; and of learning theory; as well as of the cultural, social, and political contexts in which early childhood education functions. Teachers of young children should be experts in child development. They must understand the nature of development within early childhood as well as the periods that precede and follow it. They should also be aware of variability within patterns of development, how development takes place, the antecedents of development, and the fact that different developmental domains are intertwined (Peters & Klinzing, 1990).

Teachers use instructional knowledge—theories of teaching and teaching methods—in classroom practice, planning, and evaluation. The content of instructional knowledge includes how to organize, prepare, and present instructional plans; ways to evaluate children and learning; how to recognize individual differences; methods to develop cultural awareness; an understanding of youth; management of educational resources; and establishing educational policies and procedures (Shulman, 1986).

Instructional knowledge includes content knowledge, pedagogical knowledge, and curricular knowledge. Content knowledge comes from general education as it is applied to children. Pedagogical knowledge includes both managerial and subject matter practices. Curriculum knowledge includes knowledge of program content and structure. McCarthy (1990) identified instructional knowledge as including the philosophical, historical, and psychological foundations noted here; home, school, and community relations; the creation and delivery of curriculum; health, nutrition, and safety; assessment procedures; and professional ethics. In some programs these components are offered in separate courses; in others they are integrated.

The practice component of teacher preparation programs includes field experiences, workshops, observations, simulations, practice, and student teaching. Workshops allow students to present and practice teaching techniques with different types of materials and to study the effects of these techniques on children. Classroom observation allows students to see teachers in action and relate observations of practice to theory. In simulations, students play a hypothetical role in a simple, controlled situation. Obser-

Instructional knowledge

Practice

Teachers in early childhood education need to be aware of the history and traditions of their field; of principles of child growth and development; and of learning theory; as well as of the cultural, social, and political contexts in which early childhood education functions.

Unfortunately, the profession of early childhood education has only limited influence on the nature of teacher preparation or teaching practice.

vation and student teaching are always provided in teacher education programs; other forms of practice may not be.

Field experiences can improve teacher candidates' performances as they learn about the importance of teacher-pupil relationships and observe children in a variety of circumstances (Borrowman, 1965). Field experiences, unfortunately, may also negatively affect attitudes and behaviors of candidates, who may become more authoritarian, rigid, controlling, restrictive, impersonal, and custodial; and less student centered, accepting, and humanistic, if this is what they experience in the field (Hull, Baker, Kyle, & Good, 1982; Peck & Tucker, 1973; Zeichner, 1980). Student teaching, considered the most important element in the preparation of teachers (Brimfield & Leonard, 1983), can have similar negative and positive results (Hull, Baker, Kyle, & Good, 1982; Zeichner 1980).

Several problems are intrinsic in student teaching and related field experiences. The university supervisor and cooperating teacher's responsibilities are unclear and often overlap (Grimmett & Ratzlaff, 1986; Applegate & Lasley, 1982, 1984). Cooperating teachers have the most influence in the student teaching experience. However, they are practice-oriented and do not always depend on research and theory to make generalizations about practice.

In feedback sessions with their cooperating teachers, student teachers receive very little evaluation of behavior or statements of reasons to justify their practice (Griffin et al., 1983). Discussions focus on an individual child or problem in the classroom. Feiman-Nemser and Buchmann (1985) also found this to be the case in their study of a student teacher who failed to learn ways to develop and extend content. They cite the cooperating teacher's failure to give appropriate feedback as the cause. Unfortunately, O'Neal (1983) found that the university supervisors' feedback was similar to that of the cooperating teachers.

Other limits to the quality of the student teaching experience can include lack of exposure to models of teaching that use rigorous analysis and collegiality, provision of poor feedback by cooperating teachers and supervisors, and university supervisors' failure to spend adequate time with student teachers (Saracho, 1993).

A number of strategies have been designed to deal with these problems. Some teacher education programs develop reflective habits in their student teachers by focusing on the student teachers and the university supervisors instead of the cooperating teachers (Adler & Roth, 1985; Korthagen, 1985; Zeichner & Liston, 1987). Carter (1987) feels cooperating teachers could be trained to analyze their teaching and supervision techniques. Bird (1984) suggests supervising student teaching within a larger school improvement context where reflection and critical analysis of teaching are recompensed. Little (1987) proposes that schools make provisions for student teachers to have access to shared understandings.

In order for student teaching to be of the most value to education students, schools must accept their role as a reflective and self-renewing institution where student teachers become socialized. Ideal places for student teaching are needed to accomplish the goal of helping to empower the profession through well-educated and well-socialized new teachers.

Program evaluation and modification

All teacher education programs have procedures for evaluation and modification. Some of these are quite formal, such as the National Council for Accreditation of Teacher Education (NCATE) evaluations, and assessments by certification agencies, as described by McCarthy in Part I of this volume. Other less formal and less holistic forms of evaluation are also used, ranging from student evaluation of courses to assessments by hiring agents and program alumni. Some universities also evaluate all programs periodically. The results of these evaluations can be used to modify programs.

A variety of groups have called for reforms in teacher education. These have led to reconceptualization of programs and creation of innovative approaches. At their best, such approaches lead to new ways of preparing teachers; at their worst, they lead to rearrangement of the status quo. Unfortunately, new programs too often reflect public relations approaches or the separation of teacher education from the institution's tenured faculty.

Conclusion

Early childhood education is a diverse field, and early childhood teachers represent a diverse population. No single type of program serves all children; no single type or level of preparation is reflected by all teachers in the field. Given the growing number of early childhood programs, greater attention needs to be given not only to expanding opportunities for early childhood teacher education, but also to improving teacher preparation and the conditions under which they work.

Unfortunately, the profession of early childhood education has only limited influence on the nature of teacher preparation or teaching practice. Teacher certification standards are established by state education authorities with little input from early childhood practitioners (Spodek, Davis, & Saracho, 1983). NAEYC is cooperating with NCATE to establish criteria for accrediting teacher education programs, but this is still a minor influence on a voluntary process. In addition, standards for child care staff qualifications are established by state licensing agencies (Spodek & Saracho, 1990) and differ markedly by state.

The question remains: Is there an adequate knowledge base for early childhood practice that can serve as a foundation for professional practice? Such a base must be grounded in research, must use the practical knowledge gathered by teachers, and must reflect the theoretical knowledge from both child development and education studies. The material surveyed here represents the beginning of the framework for such a knowledge base. Efforts must be made to see that it is more fully articulated and expanded as NAEYC works toward a coordinated system of early childhood professional development opportunities.

Bibliography

Adler, S., & Roth, R. (1985). *Critical inquiry in teacher preparation.* Paper presented at the annual meeting of the Association of Teacher Educators, Chicago.

Almy, M. (1975). *The early childhood educator at work.* New York: McGraw-Hill.

Applegate, J.H. (1987). Teacher candidate selection: An overview. *Journal of Teacher Education, 38*(2), 2–6.

Applegate, J.H., & Lasley, T.J. (1982). Cooperating teachers' problems with pre-service field experience students. *Journal of Teacher Education, 33*(2), 15–18.

Applegate, J.H., & Lasley, T.J. (1984). Cooperating teachers' problems with preservice field experience students. *Teacher Education, 24,* 70–82.

Bird, T. (1984). *Propositions regarding the analysis and supervision of teaching.* Paper presented to the Loveland, Colorado, School Administrators Workshop, Vail, CO.

Borrowman, M.L. (1965). *Teacher education in America.* New York: Teachers College Press.

Bowman, B. (1990). Issues in recruitment, selection, and retention of early childhood teachers. In B. Spodek & O.N. Saracho (Eds.), *Early childhood teacher preparation: Yearbook in early childhood, Vol. 1* (pp. 153–175). New York: Teachers College Press.

Brimfield, R., & Leonard, R. (1983). The student teaching experience: A time to consolidate one's perceptions. *College Student Journal, 17,* 401–406.

Carter, K. (1987). *University of Arizona cooperative teacher project: An interim report to OERI, Department of Education.* Tucson: University of Arizona.

Clark, C. (1988). Teacher preparation contributions of research on teacher thinking. *Educational Researcher, 17,* 5–12.

Evans, R., & Saracho, O.N. (Eds.). (1992). *Early childhood teacher education: An international perspective.* London: Gordon and Breach.

Feiman-Nemser, S., & Buchmann, M. (1985, February). *On what is learned in student teaching: Appraising the experience.* Paper presented at the annual meeting of the American Association of Colleges of Teacher Education, Chicago.

Gillett, M. (1973). Introduction to new directions. In J.A. Laska and M. Gillett (Eds.), *Foundation studies in education: Justifications and new directions* (pp. 264–282). Metuchen, NJ: Scarecrow Press.

Griffin, G., Barnes, S., Defino, M., Edwards, S., Hukill, H., & O'Neal, S. (1983). *Clinical preservice teacher education: Final report of a descriptive study.* Austin: University of Texas, Research and Development Center for Teacher Education.

Grimmett, P., & Ratzlaff, H. (1986). Expectations for the cooperating teacher's role. *Journal of Teacher Education, 37*(6), 41–50.

Hull, R., Baker, R., Kyle, J., & Good, R. (Eds.). (1982). *Research on student teaching: A question of transfer.* Eugene: University of Oregon, Division of Teacher Education. (ERIC Document Reproduction Service No. ED 223 561)

Katz, L.G. (1969). *Teaching in preschools: Roles and goals.* Urbana, IL: ERIC Clearinghouse on Early Childhood Education.

Korthagen, F. (1985). *Reflective thinking as a basis for teacher education.* Paper presented at the annual meeting of the American Association of Colleges of Teacher Education.

Lewin & Associates. (n.d.). *The state of teacher education, 1977.* Washington, DC: U.S. Department of Health, Education and Welfare.

Little, J.W. (1987). Teachers as colleagues. In V. Richardson-Koehler (Ed.), *Educators handbook* (pp. 491–518). New York: Longman.

McCarthy, J. (1990). The content of early childhood programs: Pedagogy. In B. Spodek & O.N. Saracho (Eds.), *Early childhood teacher education: Yearbook in early childhood education, Vol. 1* (pp. 82–101). New York: Teachers College Press.

National Association for the Education of Young Children. (1984). *NAEYC position statement on nomenclature, salaries, benefits, and the status of the profession.* Washington, DC: Author.

O'Neal, S. (1983). *Supervision of student teachers: Feedback and evaluation.* Austin: University of Texas, Research and Development Center for Teacher Education.

Peck, R.F., & Tucker, J.A. (1973). Research on teacher education. In R.M.W. Travers, (Ed.), *Second handbook of research on teaching.* Chicago: Rand McNally.

Peters, D.L., & Klinzing, D.G. (1990). The content of early childhood education programs: Child development. In B. Spodek & O.N. Saracho (Eds.), *Early childhood teacher education: Yearbook in early childhood teacher education, Vol. 1* (pp. 67–81). New York: Teachers College Press.

Powell, D.R., & Dunn, L. (1990). Non-baccalaureate teacher education in early childhood education. In B. Spodek & O.N. Saracho (Eds.), *Early childhood teacher education: Yearbook in early childhood education, Vol. 1* (pp. 45–66). New York: Teachers College Press.

Ryans, D.G. (1960). *Characteristics of teachers.* Washington, DC: American Council on Education.

Saracho, O.N. (1993). Preparing teachers for early childhood programs in the United States. In B. Spodek, *Handbook of research on the education of young children* (pp. 412–427). New York: Macmillan.

Saracho, O.N., & Spodek, B. (1983). The preparation of teachers for bilingual bicultural early childhood classes. In O.N. Saracho & B. Spodek (Eds.), *Understanding the multicultural experience in early childhood education* (pp. 125–146). Washington, DC: NAEYC.

Shulman, L.S. (1986). Those who understand: Knowledge growth in teaching. *Educational Researcher, 15*(2), 4–14.

Skinner, A.F. (1968). Teacher-training and the foundational studies. *Teacher Education, 19*(1), 26–38.

Spodek, B. (Ed.). (1993). *Handbook of research on the education of young children.* New York: Macmillan.

Spodek, B., Davis, M.D., & Saracho, O.N. (1983). Early childhood teacher education and certification. *Journal of Teacher Education, 34*(5), 50–52.

Spodek, B., & Saracho, O.N. (1990). Preparing early childhood teachers for the twenty-first century: A look to the future. In B. Spodek & O.N. Saracho (Eds.), *Yearbook in early childhood education, Vol. 1* (pp. 45–66). New York: Teachers College Press.

Spodek, B., Saracho, O.N., & Peters, D.L. (Eds.). (1989). *Professionalism and the early childhood practitioner.* New York: Teachers College Press.

VanderVen, K. (1988). Pathways to professional effectiveness for early childhood educators. In B. Spodek, O.N. Saracho, and D.L. Peters (Eds.), *Professionalism and the early childhood practitioner* (pp. 137–160). New York: Teachers College Press.

Zeichner, K.M. (1980). Myth and realities: Field-based experiences in pre-service teacher education. *Journal of Teacher Education, 31*(6), 45–55.

Zeichner, K.M., & Liston, D.P. (1987). Teaching student teachers to reflect. *Harvard Educational Review, 57*(1), 23–48.

Professional Development: A Contextual Model

Karen VanderVen

A positive relationship exists between prepared practitioners, program quality, and improved developmental outcomes for young children. Research (Goelman, 1992) reveals that when young children are served by prepared staff in stimulating, safe, sensitive, and flexible environments, children exhibit enhanced cognitive ability (richer language, higher test scores) and enhanced social skills (increased social interaction, greater social competence, increased responsiveness).

Only a dynamic and revolutionary approach to early childhood education professionalism will assure that the field can continue to support children and families in this way. *Professionalism* is the ability to plan knowledgeably and competently to make a sustained difference: to diagnose and analyze situations, to select the most appropriate interventions, to apply them skillfully, and to describe why they were selected (Katz, 1984; VanderVen, 1988). *Professionalization* refers to the degree to which a field is advancing toward meeting recognized criteria for a profession (VanderVen, 1988).

In order to achieve the goal of professionalism for all, the nature of the field—the knowledge, skills, and attributes required for practice; and the context of professionalization—must be examined. Simply knowing what works is insufficient. Two questions are pursued here: What is the fundamental nature of knowledge in early childhood education? What other kinds of knowledge are necessary to continue to advance the field? A contextual model for professional development is proposed to clarify the nature of work with young children and their families.

The core curriculum for professional preparation of teachers and caregivers of young children in the United States and Canada (Peters, Kelly, VanderVen, Mattingly, & Morris, 1982; Goelman, 1992) generally includes

- child and human development theory and empirical knowledge, normal and exceptional
- environmental design and physical setting
- curriculum, program design, and activity programming
- activities of daily living and routines
- communication skills
- relationship strategies
- health and safety
- specialty areas, e.g., multiculturalism, child abuse
- family-centered practice—parent education, parent involvement, family intervention strategies

> *Only a dynamic and revolutionary approach to early childhood education professionalism will assure that the field can continue to support children and families.*

Core knowledge for direct practice

- special skills such as observation and assessment
- community relationships, advocacy, service coordination
- professional issues: ethics, professional development

The clarity of these ideas supports the notion of a professional concerned with promoting positive development.

Interestingly, closely related fields, e.g. child and youth work and gerontology, consider the same core areas as the essence of their emerging professions. One possibility is to integrate professionalization efforts to work toward a unified field that combines various aspects of nurturing and educational/therapeutic interventions across the life span (VanderVen, 1992). Early childhood education would be a specialty. Such a broad-based profession would be neither age- nor setting-specific, as are most other professions. An advantage of such an approach would be formation of a larger constituent group. However, it might be more difficult to advocate for or focus on young children. Another alternative is to move early childhood forward on the basis of a new and different concept of a profession.

One possibility is to integrate professionalization efforts to work toward a unified field that combines various aspects of nurturing and educational/therapeutic interventions across the life span.

Core knowledge for indirect practice

What do practitioners need to know beyond this fundamental core of direct practice knowledge? What do those who advance the conceptual aspects of the field, who act as change agents, need to know? What content and preparation are needed for *transformational* as well as more traditional *transactional* leadership (Kuhnert & Lewis, 1989)? Both components are needed in the early childhood professionalization effort.

Transactional leaders have first-line administrative knowledge and skills in areas such as budget development, physical plant management, parent programming, staff development and supervision, and staff and program evaluation.

Professional development should promote intrinsic motivation so that practitioners will be eager to acquire and generate new knowledge.

Transformational leaders are concerned with vision—long-term planning, changing intransigent systems, building meta-theory and expanded practice models, and the like. Without these powerful leaders, full professionalism is impossible. These leaders need to understand

- first- and second-order change, and how to attain both
- chaos theory, given that situations are subject to chaotic phenomena
- paradoxical results, to be able to anticipate unexpected results from actions and interventions
- strategic thinking, including game and decision theory
- futurism, including strategies and models for prediction
- marketing, including strategic marketing models
- evolution, including notions of the continuing process of human evolution
- theory building, so that practice-based theory is developed and tested against current practice

The nature of knowledge subsumed in early childhood practice is a philosophical, epistemological issue, with tremendous bearing on the kind of profession that the field can become. Although there are similarities with other human service fields, the kind of knowledge needed to work with young children is quite different. Knowledge in early childhood is context-driven, and rapid information processing is often required to make a practice decision. Thus, development of an epistemology embracing the nature of this unique knowledge, and integrating this into the design of professional preparation systems, could radically enhance the development of full professionalism. Several aspects of this knowledge might be considered.

Ill-structured knowledge. Most knowledge needed for early childhood practice is neither linear nor sequentially organized. Rather, it fits Spiro's notion of ill-structured knowledge in that it is chaotic, non-linear, and subject to recursion effects (Jones, 1990). This reality must be acknowledged in professional preparation programs. Practitioners work with many individual personalities in a multi-level, shifting context. A simple array of interventions from which to select is inadequate. Early childhood educators must know how to quickly access a given circumstance, how to select the most appropriate intervention, and how to anticipate possible outcomes.

Information theory. Acting from a single perspective and failing to take context into account are practices followed by many unprepared early childhood personnel (VanderVen, 1988). In contrast, Langer (1989) describes *mindfulness*, in which a person takes context into account when making a decision and acting. In order to prepare practitioners to deal with ill-structured knowledge, and to encourage mindful practice, effective professional development programs must consider how adult students take in information, what information is taken in, how it is sorted, what is retrieved, and how it is reconfigured.

The nature of knowledge

Heuristics and meta-cognition. In addition to core knowledge and skills, practitioners must be aware of viable "rules of thumb" for problem solving, or heuristics, and to be aware that among these are their own vicarious selection processes in perception, learning, and other relevant areas (Wimsatt, 1986). Consider the relevance of heuristics of meta-cognition in education: awareness not only of what one knows, but the cognitive strategies one uses to deal with this knowledge. With such strategies, the knowledge base underlying practice is strengthened.

Spiral curriculum. Another area to consider is how to deliver and develop knowledge and skill in a content area that sequentially has more depth and complexity. Application of the spiral curriculum concept will foster professional development activities that reflect levels of practice from novice to expert. This in turn can ensure that there is a push toward the highest level of practice, and that the field develops and retains these professionals.

Artistry. Artistry often has been viewed as a nebulous aspect of practice that should be discounted. A sharper vision of artistry (Schon, 1987) proposes that artistry is a recognizable aspect of any profession, particularly those involving people. Several pertinent issues include how to articulate artistry, how to prepare for its use, and how to identify the relationship between artistry and specific practice skills.

Relationships between theory and practice

Theory can be translated into practice, and, conversely, practice into theory. Practitioners must know how to do both. Traditionally, theory has been presented with the expectation that students would translate it into practice and vice versa (VanderVen, 1993). In order to better articulate the ties between practice and theory, early childhood professional preparation programs must recognize that knowledge is generated from practice that is conceptualized and related to other theories; and theory is translated into application by a reciprocal, several-step process.

Constructivism. Students should be prepared to become "practitioner scientists" who reflect on their practice and articulate their practice-based theories. The idea of constructivist learning and teaching (Fosnot, 1989) that is applied to design of learning experiences for children has similar implications for preparing adults. Practitioners must be encouraged to systematically review what they do, conceptualize their ideas into practice principles and theories, test them against other relevant theories, and apply them in new practice. Constructivism that is not tested against the best of what is already known, however, will fall short. This raises the necessity for the reciprocal relationship between theory and practice. The process of using practice as a basis for formulating theory must tie in with known theory, not simply be conceptualized upward from direct practice in isolation.

Linkages between the academic and applications. Practitioner preparation and knowledge generation/dissemination are enhanced by forging links within the professional between academics and service personnel. Knowledge generated in practice (service) needs to be recorded and processed (academic); theory (academic) needs to be tested in the direct setting (service). The notion of specially trained practice teachers who can formally encourage this activity is one way of better connecting the academic and practice sectors; a comprehensive model for bridging the gap needs to be enacted (VanderVen, 1993).

A comprehensive view of knowledge reveals many other factors that impinge on professional preparation and practice.

Effects of cognitive and social styles. Warmth, sensitivity, and flexibility are traits of effective teachers. Cognitive style, such as field dependence and independence, also has great implications for professional development (Saracho, 1988). Other factors may also be related to increasing the quality of the early childhood work force.

Intrinsic motivation. Efforts to professionalize early childhood practice heretofore have tended to focus on aspects related to extrinsic motivation, e.g., salaries and working conditions. These are absolutely crucial, but management theory suggests that these factors are even more potent when combined with activities that promote intrinsic motivation. Intrinsic motivation—the internal incentive to learn and develop new knowledge, attitudes, and skills—is a crucial attribute for early childhood practitioners. Professional development should promote intrinsic motivation so that practitioners will be eager to acquire and generate new knowledge, will persist in the face of frustration, can solve the problems they encounter, and are prepared to make a significant difference in the field.

Curiosity. Related to motivation, yet often overlooked in considering professionalism, is learner curiosity. The burning desire to learn new things is often lacking among early childhood students and practitioners. How often are in-service sessions presented to stolid audiences that never ask a question? One of the greatest barriers to professionalism is the lack of curiosity within many in the field, which tends to keep staff "stuck" in their usual ways of viewing and doing things. New ways to recruit curious people to early childhood education, and activities that promote and enhance curiosity, are sorely needed.

Cognitive dissonance. Resistance to new ideas and approaches is endemic in the field, particularly among those at the novice and initial stages of professional development, where the critical mass of practitioners reside (VanderVen, 1988). *Cognitive dissonance* refers to the tendency to reject information that is incompatible with one's world view and to reconfigure incoming information to accommodate that world view. Practitioners must be encouraged to change their mindsets in the face of new information that may challenge deeply entrenched and personalized ways of thinking (Tittnich, 1985). Failure to continue to learn can perpetuate inept, nonprofessional practice (Katz, 1984).

Other factors affecting professionalism

Failure to continue to learn can perpetuate inept, nonprofessional practice.

Early childhood is horizontally integrated across the domains of care, education, and development, unlike fields such as nursing and social work which are integrated vertically in a life-span perspective.

Marketing mentality. Until many practitioners feel eminently comfortable with the notion of marketing, from strategic planning to positively promoting their work and their field, attainment of professionalism will be greatly hindered by unproductive humility and non-proactive mindsets (VanderVen, 1984). Assumption of an appropriate marketing mentality seems to be associated with the stage of professional development and the ability to embrace broader, less traditional notions. Professional preparation must necessarily include anticipatory socialization for the assumption of a marketing mentality.

Level of intelligence. The field should make every effort to recruit the most intelligent young people. This will contribute to optimal utilization of all levels of preparation, enhance the knowledge base of the field, and ultimately advance professionalism. Influential-stage practitioners are challenged to come up with innovative ways to do this and to reduce the "brain drain" from early childhood education (Katz, 1988), which is perhaps a greater barrier to professionalism than the field dares to think.

The contextual model for early childhood

The criteria for a profession—in a traditional or sociological sense, and the degree to which early childhood meets them—have been identified by others (VanderVen, 1985). It is prudent to accommodate the recognized models of a profession, but also to pioneer in the development of newer, more appropriate models, in an effort to further advance early childhood professionalism.

The contextual model of a profession (VanderVen, 1992), is one such possibility. This model complements the traditional linear model that is concerned primarily with structural aspects of early childhood education rather than the social nature of the work. It addresses some of the problems that early childhood encounters when viewed solely within the linear model, such as that it is age specific, that it straddles the two domains of care and education, and that it deals with non-linear dynamics and events. Some characteristics of linear and contextual professions are compared in Table 5.

Incorporation of the contextual model into the early childhood field would help address the issues of horizontal and vertical integration—how the field relates to other professions and to people in other age groups. Early childhood is horizontally integrated across the domains of care, education, and development, unlike fields such as nursing and social work which are integrated vertically in a life-span perspective.

The debate in early childhood about the relationship between education and care can be addressed by considering this: the service early childhood educators provide is to promote development, which combines both care and education.

EDUCATION + CARE = DEVELOPMENT

The relative balance between education and care depends on the age and maturity of the child. For infants, care and education are intertwined. As

Table 5. Models of Professions

Linear Profession	Contextual Profession
Specialized, highly structured interventions	Generic, situationally applied
Knowledge sources emphasize own discipline	Knowledge sources multidisciplinary
Knowledge sequentially organized, linear	Knowledge dynamic, non-linear
Primarily theory/research base	Practice and theory base
Provides specialized service to persons of all ages	Provides service to targeted age groups but promotes connections with others as part of service
Focus on specific outcomes	Focus on process toward varied outcomes
Focus on specific syndromes or conditions	Holistic focus on overall development
Integration of client experience not part of service	Serves to integrate client (child) experience
Traditional professional/client distance	Professional relationship de-emphasizes distance
Service less influenced by context	Nature of service highly context driven
Uni- or multidisciplinary with clear role locations	Interdisciplinary and transdisciplinary aspects
Prescribed knowledge and skill base; intuition and artistry present but de-emphasized	Intuition and artistry provide frame for knowledge and skill utilization

children mature, care and education are less integrated. By school age, care and education are delivered by separate institutions. Care and education intersect in early childhood, so most settings provide care with an educational focus, and education with a nurturant aspect. The goal of both is to promote positive development, so perhaps the dilemma can be solved if the focus is on development. The field of professional practice might therefore be called *early childhood development* and practitioners might be called *developmentalists* rather that caregivers or teachers.

Professional preparation within the contextual model

Transfer of knowledge and skills is the purpose of professional preparation, yet designs for professional development models rarely apply what is known about this transfer. Transfer is more likely to occur if support is introduced long before the targeted learning experience, is included in the strategies used to promote learning, and ends long after. Variables that enhance the transfer of knowledge and skills are outlined in Table 6. Transfer is more likely to occur as an increasing number of these variables are included in an individual's professional preparation.

Variables enhancing transfer of knowledge and skills

Variables enhancing transfer of knowledge and skills
- Overall culture of professional development setting supports new learning and application to practice.
- Activities address participant values about learning and various practices.
- Faculty show personal interest in learners as appropriate to situation.
- Appropriate practice is positively demonstrated.
- Concurrent (accompanying cognitive content) and massed (following formal "classroom instruction") field work are both included.
- Practice is supervised by a person experienced in the same field.
- Skills are practiced (with supervision) to point of overtraining.
- Participants are encouraged to consider applications of skills in different contexts and to anticipate both barriers and supports to applications.
- Content offers optimal disparity (Tittnich, 1991)—it is neither too familiar nor too different.
- Participants are involved, as appropriate, in selecting content and teaching strategies.
- Teaching strategies relate to learning preferences and styles.
- Cooperative, collaborative, and peer teaching methods are included in instructional methods.
- Teaching methods closely approximate the application into practice and tend to be nontraditional. For example:
  - *Guided imagery* allows practitioners to visualize the situation and review options for response (Tittnich, 1991).
  - *Case studies* allow the practitioner to identify with real-life situations.
  - *Simulation* allows for actual practice in replicated, real situations. Simulation is effective to the degree it is objectives-based and par-

ticipants are debriefed to encourage conceptualization of experience and review its congruence with established knowledge.

- Follow-up and maintenance activities—peer coaching, mentoring, regular feedback—occur over an extended time period.

Summary

A well-prepared, professional work force is essential to meet the needs of children and their families. The fundamental areas and nature of professional knowledge outlined here, combined with other factors that affect its application, lead to the recommendation of a contextual model of professional development.

References

Fosnot, C. (1989). *Enquiring teachers, enquiring learners.* New York: Teachers College Press.

Goelman, H. (1992). *Visions of program revision: A report on the Early Childhood Education Review Project.* University of British Columbia: Center for the Study of Curriculum and Instruction.

Jones, R. (1990). To criss-cross in every direction or why hypermedia works. *Academic Computing, 30,* 20–21.

Katz, L. (1984). The professional early childhood teacher. *Young Children, 38*(5), 3–11.

Katz, L. (1988). Where is early childhood education as a profession? In B. Spodek, O. Saracho, & D. Peters (Eds.), *Professionalism and the early childhood educator* (pp. 75–83). New York: Columbia University Press.

Kuhnert, K., & Lewis, P. (1989). Transactional and transformational leadership: A constructive developmental analysis. In W. Rosenbach & R. Taylor (Eds.), *Contemporary issues in leadership.* Second Edition. Boulder, CO: Westview Press.

Langer, E . (1989). *Mindfulness.* Reading, MA: Addison-Wesley.

Peters, D., Kelly, C., VanderVen, K., Mattingly, M., & Morris, M. (1982). Principles and guidelines for early childhood personnel preparation programs. *Child Care Quarterly, 11*(3), 221–244.

Saracho, O. (1988). Cognitive style and early childhood practice. In B. Spodek, O. Saracho, & D. Peters (Eds.), *Professionalism and the early childhood educator* (pp. 173–188). New York: Columbia University Press.

Schon, D. (1987). *Educating the reflective practitioner.* San Francisco: Jossey-Bass.

Tittnich, E. (1985). Training that takes. In K. VanderVen & E. Tittnich (Eds.), *Competent caregivers: Competent children* (pp. 47–55). New York: Haworth.

Tittnich, E. (1991). *The impact of memory in cognitive and affective approaches to training child care workers.* Paper delivered at the International Federation of Education Communities Seminar of Experts in Training, Neurim, Israel.

VanderVen, K. (1984). Barriers to an effective marketing stance in child care. *Children in Contemporary Society, 17*(2), 43–56.

VanderVen, K. (1985). "You've come a long way, baby": The evolution and significance of caregiving. In K. VanderVen & E. Tittnich (Eds.), *Competent caregivers: Competent children* (pp. 3–12). New York: Haworth.

VanderVen, K. (1988). Pathways to professionalism. In B. Spodek, O. Saracho, & D. Peters (Eds.), *Professionalism and the early childhood educator* (pp. 137–160). New York: Columbia University Press.

VanderVen, K. (1992). Developmental care: A proposal for a new profession whose time is coming! *Journal of Child and Youth Care, 7*(4), 3–38.

VanderVen, K. (1993). Advancing child and youth care: A model for integrating theory and practice through connecting education, training and the service system. *Child and Youth Care Forum, 22*(4), 263–284.

Wimsatt, W. (1986). Heuristics and the study of human behavior. In D. Fiske & R. Shweder (Eds.), *Meta-theory in social science* (pp. 293–314). Chicago: University of Chicago Press.

PART III

Effective Professional Development Strategies

Learning is a lifelong pursuit for early childhood educators—professionals engage in learning and at the same time nurture young children's and their colleagues' desire to learn. Content and teaching strategies are intertwined in professional development just as they are with young children. The concept of a career lattice and the vision of continuous professional growth are similarly intertwined. Expertise is gained—and refined daily— all along the various career paths.

The need for practical, relevant, transferable knowledge about effective professional practice echoes through Part III. Perspectives from research and experience describe how the profession's knowledge base and competencies are achieved at different points on the career lattice. Contributors highlight delivery mechanisms that increase accessibility to the professional development system to assure the field's diversity and congruence with the families and children served. These insights provoke inspiration to move NAEYC's framework from concept into action. Embedded within Part III are numerous recommendations that can improve the day-to-day skills of professionals who are engaged in fostering each other's learning.

The domains of content and strategies are bridged by **Edward Greene**, Director of Programs at the Center for Educational Programs. For many years, Greene has encouraged adults to grow in their expertise in early childhood education. He challenges current thinking and advocates inclusion of critical areas—communication and collaboration, diversity, observation and assessment, and human interactions—in state-of-the-art professional development programs.

David P. Weikart, President of the High/Scope Educational Research Foundation, has been exploring various aspects of high-quality early childhood programs, including staff development, for more than 30 years. Among the Foundation's activities are the Training-of-Trainers Project; the Lead Training Program for key teaching staff; and workshops on curriculum, computers, and movement. Weikart shares new research identifying components of effective professional development programs for those already working in group settings with young children.

Diversity characterizes every aspect of the field, including strategies for professional development. One gap in the array of possibilities is addressed by California's unique, comprehensive video program for caregivers of infants and toddlers. This innovative curriculum is described by **J. Ronald Lally, Carol Lou Young-Holt, and Peter Mangione** from the Far West Laboratory, developers of the materials. Success of this and similar efforts indi-

Diversity characterizes every aspect of the field, including strategies for professional development.

cate that emerging technologies play a promising role in accessibility of professional growth opportunities.

Effective strategies for engaging family child care providers in learning more about their responsibilities are recommended by **Nancy Cohen** and **Kathy Modigliani.** Cohen, Research Associate at the Yale Bush Center, and Modigliani, Director of the Family Child Care Project at Wheelock College, draw firsthand insights from the Family-to-Family Project experiences.

Reflections on Head Start's comprehensive system of continuous training for staff at various stages in their careers provide a wealth of information. **Barbara L. Wolfe,** formerly early intervention specialist with the Great Lakes Access Project in Portage, Wisconsin, and currently faculty at a four-year college, reviews the results of a survey of Head Start staff. She describes how leaders of professional development opportunities can facilitate transfer of learning into daily practice, and reveals several important points for supervisors and group facilitators to consider.

Paula Jorde Bloom, an expert in program leadership at National-Louis University, outlines The Early Childhood Leadership and Advocacy Program model. Supervisors and administrators of programs for young children will be especially interested in how this model improves teaching practices in programs and professional leadership capacities.

A vision of comprehensive, continuous professional development opportunities for school-age child care personnel is extended by **Susan O'Connor,** Project Associate at Wellesley's School-Age Child Care Project. She reviews the state of this relatively young field and offers ambitious insights for increased professionalism for those who choose this career path.

Elizabeth Jones concludes with yet another insightful professional development strategy. She urges the field to improve practice at all entry points on the career lattice by recognizing the knowledge that adults bring to every learning situation. Betty's approach to facilitating adult learning captures the imaginative, curious spirit that exemplifies early childhood education.

Part III crystallizes the notion that everyone in early childhood education continues to learn through observations and experiences. An articulated, coordinated professional development system, then, must bring together the field's growing knowledge base and diverse learning opportunities. In charting the system's course, the emphasis shifts from an outdated, often haphazard *training* perspective to a lifelong, constructivist commitment to *professional development.*

In charting the system's course, the emphasis shifts from an outdated, often haphazard training perspective to a life-long, constructivist commitment to professional development.

State-of-the-Art Professional Development

Edward Greene

Early childhood educators serve in a variety of roles and provide an array of services to children and families. Public understanding of who early childhood educators are and what each person does, along with each professional's self-perceptions, appear to be gaining clarity. The capacity to create and deliver state-of-the-art professional development opportunities is steadily increasing. Early childhood policies, practices, and human relationships merit further attention because of their impact on the process of professional development.

This field encompasses a complexity of private and public sectors; governmental and non-governmental agencies; and a variety of programs, funding streams, and populations. Understanding relationships between the various parts—center-based and home-based; for-profits and nonprofits; programs for working parents and low-income families; infant, toddler, preschool, kindergarten, and primary personnel; competency-based, two-year, and four-year professional preparation programs—is a daunting task.

One of the challenges for early childhood is to better define professionalism. A cadre of professionals, including administrators, policymakers, and direct service providers are striving to communicate effectively and work collaboratively to develop coordinated, articulated programs and a meaningful career development track. Gaps are being identified and bridged through NAEYC's National Institute for Early Childhood Professional Development conferences and publications.

Effective communication skills enable professionals to maximize the benefits of environments for young children as well as to build relationships among children's homes, programs, and the various sectors that provide services. Communication and collaboration are essential as the Institute moves forward in its quest to translate NAEYC's conceptual framework from concept to action. Sound professional development strategies must address how adults become skilled, confident, and competent in communicating and collaborating with each other. Positive interactions should characterize the people whose behaviors children are expected to emulate.

A variety of sources are available to help adults learn how to communicate and function more effectively in organizations and in their relationships. The fields of organizational development and human resource development offer state-of-the-art information and technical assistance. Among the sources that can be used to examine institutional and interpersonal communication and collaboration are the National Training Laboratory (NTL) Institute (Reedy & Jamison, 1988), Carlson Learning Company in

Communication and collaboration

Sound professional development strategies must address how adults become skilled, confident, and competent in communicating and collaborating with each other.

Minneapolis, Minnesota, and Outward Bound Professional Development Programs, New York, New York.

Diversity

Early childhood educators must learn to use the power of diversity to solve human problems.

The ways in which professionals deal with differences are crucial to the quality of human relations. Every day, early childhood educators encounter society's diversity. Issues that must be acknowledged and affirmatively addressed include working professionally with people who speak languages other than English, issues of gender equity, immigrant populations, people with disabilities, low-income people, and people of color.

Race, class, gender, disability, economic status, and sexual preference are highly sensitive topics. *Diversity* is the word typically used to encompass inclusion and equity issues. Increasing numbers of staff development workshops address topics such as managing diversity. Business and industry engage management-level personnel in sensitivity training to help them better understand and manage people. Consider the implications if diversity is viewed as something to be managed. Does this mean that diversity causes things to be out of control and is a problem to be contained? Or is it a resource to be cultivated and used as a way to strengthen human productivity? *Managing diversity* is a phrase to be used cautiously.

People generally are socialized not to pay too much attention to differences and to focus on how everyone is alike. When teachers are asked how they handle diversity and meet the individual needs of children, the response is often, "Well, I have high expectations, so I treat everyone just alike. I don't make differentiations." Teachers who respond in this way believe that by seeing everyone as being the same, they provide fair treatment. In fact, people who treat everyone "just alike" by default interact in an uninformed manner. In adult-child relationships, the child loses out if the adult is not able to look at and listen to a child's idiosyncratic style of doing things, such as expressing needs or interest.

Differences can be observed, for example, in behaviors, beliefs, physical attributes, and socioeconomic status. Differences are not inherently wrong or negative; they can serve as tools to inform, enlighten, and contribute positively to an individual's interactions with children, families, and practitioners. Differences become a problem when judgment enters the scene. Opinions, or *differentness*, then become the emphasis. *Differentness* inflates differences into contrasting judgments that reflect an imposition of values and attitudes.

Early childhood educators must learn to use the power of diversity to solve human problems. Whether the knowledge is applied in service settings or in political and advocacy arenas, professionals must become aware of the ways in which overt or covert prejudices and "isms" creep into language, attitudes, and actions. To avoid unfair judgments, proactive approaches to diversity must replace strategies that center on reactions to differences. Conflict management, human relations, and intergroup and interpersonal relationships are closely related skills. The acquisition of knowledge and skills in these areas, and conscious and unconscious behaviors related to differences, must be addressed in state-of-the-art professional development programs in order to prepare individuals to work with diverse children and families.

Learning how to bridge the needs, experiences, goals, and interests of children and adults requires observation and assessment skills. Observation provides an opportunity to collect and share information to improve knowledge, understanding, and to plan future interventions and goals. Assessment requires the use of standards by which responses or observations can be judged.

Observation and assessment, when conducted ethically and appropriately, helps professionals communicate information about the progress and growth of programs, children, and staff. It requires, for example, the collection of objective information about what people do and say. Observations and assessments are sometimes made through using tools; some are published commercially, others are home grown.

Effective state-of-the-art professional development should promote caution and provide information and skills that will lead to the elimination of improper use of tools such as readiness tests and screening instruments. Meisels (1985) and Hilliard (1989) provide particularly useful warnings and suggestions. It is important that information collected about children (and adults) be used to inform practice and to make adjustments to the physical environment, activities, practitioner attitudes, and performance.

Hilliard (1989) describes two philosophical stances that people tend to take with regard to evaluation of student progress or acquired knowledge. One approach enables teachers and students to grow; the other keeps thinking to a minimum. The first approach asks "What do you know?" It tends to open the opportunity for children to describe what they think, how they perceive their experiences, and talk about what they are doing. The second is based on "Do you know what I know?" The adult who uses this approach has a preconceived answer that must be given by the student e.g., the "right" answer in the teacher's manual.

There is room for structured, knowledge-based activities. Social knowledge, for example, is often learned by rote and as a result of consequences associated with a response or behavior. Rules about the use of unit blocks fall into this category. Unit blocks are not to be used to hit others, or to destroy property. This information is shared by everyone in the classroom. Although children may talk about how they use blocks, or what they know about blocks, they are not allowed to use them to hit other people or destroy things.

Too often, programs and their success are based solely on scores and standardized measures. As a result, staff and families end up with very little information about what children actually know, and have less information to draw upon in order to plan for children's needs. Whether it is to

Observation and assessment

Learning how to bridge the needs, experiences, goals, and interests of children and adults requires observation and assessment skills.

benefit young children, staff, practitioners in training, volunteers, or programs in general, state-of-the-art professional development should

- help people develop skills to observe, record, and give feedback for the purpose of improvement and growth
- help adults understand that what is taught and experienced in the teaching/learning environment needs to be observed, critiqued, and reported to benefit teaching, learning, and service delivery goals

Interactions among adults and children

Early childhood educators must be prepared not only as kind and loving people; they must be planners, thinkers, and collaborators.

Education means to draw information from the learner, in contrast to pouring information into the learner. A quick review of the teaching materials in any catalog, however, would indicate that the "teaching as telling" model is still very popular with those who work with young children along with the "do you know what I know?" approach to testing and assessment. Although most staff developers say they do not promote this approach in training programs and workshops, only a few people apparently feel confident enough to implement appropriate practice in their classrooms.

Early childhood educators must be prepared not only as kind and loving people; they must be planners, thinkers, and collaborators. State-of-the-art professional development must emphasize the importance of human interactions. Preparations before children arrive, and plans for interactions among children, adults, and children and adults, must be well thought through. Attention to the area of adult/adult interaction may improve the ways in which child/child and adult/child interactions are promoted. The need for knowledge, skills, and strategies to promote teamwork, team planning, and team building is apparent throughout early childhood education.

The profession's somewhat blurred purpose, meaning, and direction is coming into focus. Professional development, policy, funding, and service delivery concerns must be viewed within the contexts in which they exist. **Professional development should value**

1. **A personal sense of self-understanding and the context of settings in which one works.** The Council for Early Childhood Professional Recognition's text, *Essentials for Child Development Associates,* examines this in its first chapter (Phillips, 1991a).

2. **Educational development as an ongoing process for children and adults.** Appropriate practices have been identified in relationship to work with children (Bredekamp, 1987); equal time must be given to adults and the context of adult learning.

3. **Examination of the environment, experiences, and daily routines.** Adult/adult and child/child interaction must be viewed as dynamics that have the potential to inform and improve practice.

4. **Opportunities for self-assessment, self-development, and self-renewal.** This is important for children as well as adults.

Eisner's observations are a fitting conclusion for this discussion.

The images of what teachers do in classrooms, how they teach and organize children and tasks, are acquired very early in a child's life. In one sense, teaching is the only profession in which professional socialization begins at age 5 or 6—when children begin school. In no other field do children have as much systematic opportunity to learn what a professional does in his or her work. Indeed, many children spend more time with their teachers than with their parents. This fact of early professional socialization should not be underestimated. Many young adults choose teaching because of their image of teachers and this image is not unrelated to what they believe being a teacher entails. Images of teaching and ways of being a teacher are internalized early in a child's life and bringing about significant changes in the ways in which teachers function requires replacing old images with new, more adequate ones. When a university teacher or education program tries to promulgate a new image of teaching, but sends its young, would-be teachers back to schools that are essentially like the ones in which they were socialized, the prospects for replacing the old ideals in the all too familiar contexts in which new teachers work is dimmed: The new wine is changed when it is poured into the old bottle. (Eisner, 1992, p. 611)

References

Bredekamp, S. (Ed.). (1987). *Developmentally appropriate practice in early childhood programs serving children from birth through age 8.* Washington, DC: NAEYC.

Eisner, E. (1992). Education reform and the ecology of schooling. In E.C. Langermann (Ed.), *Teachers College Record, 93*(4).

Hilliard, A.G. (1989). *Testing, tracking, and timing: Policies that deny equity and access.* Paper presented at the Annual Conference of the National Association for the Education of Young Children, Atlanta, GA.

Meisels, S. (1985). *Developmental screening in early childhood: A guide.* Third edition. Washington, DC: NAEYC.

Phillips, C.B. (Ed.). (1991a). *Essentials for Child Development Associates working with young children.* Washington, DC: Council for Early Childhood Professional Recognition.

Phillips, C.B. (Ed.). (1991b). *Seminar instructor's guide for the CDA Professional Preparation Program.* Washington, DC: Council for Early Childhood Professional Recognition.

Reedy, W.B., & Jamison, K. (Eds.). (1988). *Team building: Blueprints for productivity and satisfaction.* Alexandria, VA: National Institute for Applied Behavioral Science.

The Research Shows: Issues in Staff Development

David P. Weikart

Skills necessary to work successfully with children require a setting and opportunities best found in the work place.

W. Edwards Deming, creator of modern concepts of quality control and business management, had great success in applying his methods in Japan (Deming, 1986). He had less success in the United States, where short-term gains are more often rewarded than the long-term growth that he purports. Deming was often quoted as saying: "A university teaches knowledge, not skills. I have some advice for you: Get a job. Learn how it's done . . . and get paid while you learn."

Few early childhood educators would debate the need for knowledge, but the question here is how to gain the skills necessary to execute the job. "Get a job. Learn how it's done . . . ," is an oversimplification, at least in this field, but it does speak to the basic philosophy behind the High/Scope approach to staff development. Skills necessary to work successfully with children require a setting and opportunities best found in the work place.

In-service learning is thus the preferred method for gaining skills to implement High/Scope's developmentally appropriate curriculum, although an increasing number of two- and four-year colleges are adopting it as a basis for preparing students. A recent study (Epstein, 1993), examined the method's chain of training: High/Scope consultant to trainer, trainer to teacher, teacher to child-in-classroom. Results indicate that the training sequence works, with positive impact evident at each stage. When compared to children in other high-quality classrooms, the children in the High/

Adults seem amazed as they learn to share control with children.

Scope groups perform at a significantly higher level on important developmental variables.

High/Scope continues to consider how to improve its professional development system. Three areas stand out in the Foundation's research: realities of work in the field, integration of knowledge into practice, and principles of adult learning.

Workplace realities

Working with young children is an exciting challenge, but not without some typical problems. Teachers in the field are not well treated. Many are criticized by administrators, parents, or other staff. As a result, they often are afraid of each other and of outsiders. Institutions seem to encourage a great deal of talk but provide little incentive to act. Expectations of many administrators create the impression of unrealistic work loads and unachievable goals. Together these pressures create a situation where continuous staff development is difficult.

Teachers seem to know about child development and appropriate learning and teaching strategies, but observations in classroom and training indicate that this knowledge is applied inconsistently. Teachers seem to be too literal, taking ideas at face value and applying them without regard to the needs of children and families. Make-and-take workshops may be exciting, but often lead to development of inappropriate materials. Philosophy discussions may be written down and applied in settings where the ideas are disruptive.

In addition, most teacher-child interactions appear to be about management issues such as children's behaviors that permit teachers to control the group. Perhaps this issue is central, for it is key to the type of curriculum employed. Despite a general commitment to developmentally appropriate practices, sharing control of the classroom apparently is the most difficult thing for staff to accept.

Integrating knowledge into practice

As teachers become involved in their own long-term learning, certain persistent issues emerge. First, they become aware that children are the same—everywhere. As they observe children on videotape, in their own classrooms, and in other classrooms where they are learning, they see the stages of development exhibited in common behaviors and responses. The differences that emerge are specific to culture and language. Teachers who have this understanding are ready to permit the transfer of knowledge, methods, procedures, and specific skills among themselves. It is always the children who, in response to the curriculum and a reduction of behavior problems, create within the teacher the openness to change.

The training process is cyclical. Adults learn best and are willing to change most easily when the processes to be changed are impersonal and at a distance from their own philosophy. For example, in the High/Scope sequence, learning to arrange the classroom in meaningful child-centered areas is easiest; labeling objects, supplies, and toys on shelves is next. These steps make teaching easier and are quickly integrated into practice. The impact on children is obvious as evidenced by reduced behavior problems.

Asking children to make choices and then supporting their choices is often more threatening, and learning to share control of the learning process is next. Learning to see and understand the developmental processes in individual child behavior that undergird daily classroom practice and individual child learning is most difficult. Effective training must travel this distance of uncertain length for each participant—from the safe impersonal to the dangerous personal; from the certain observable concrete to the uncertain judgmental abstract; from the teacher as monarch to the teacher as co-participant.

Lack of knowledge is not usually at issue. Many staff are well-educated. Integration of knowledge into practice is the key. The language of developmentally appropriate practice has entered the lexicon of the field, but its application with children is still lacking. Staff generally voice a commitment to child choice and independent decision-making. Yet many programs are characterized by teacher-led subject units, commercial games, or a strong emphasis on inappropriate age-related skill expectations.

Adult learning principles

One of the most important things High/Scope has learned in working with staff from all kinds of agencies is that learning takes time: time to adjust to ideas, time to observe change in children, time to try out ideas with the children in their own groups, and time to take things step by step and not to feel forced to venture into uncharted ground. It takes about a year to incorporate the ideas, and then several more years for the curriculum to become "owned" by the participant so that it ceases to be High/Scope's curriculum and becomes her or his own curriculum.

Therefore, staff development needs to be distributed over time. It is easier to apply a series of small steps one at a time, rather than to attempt everything at once. Out of the experience of wrestling with the initial problems of application of new ideas comes the platform to build next stages. Careful sequencing of issues to be learned and applied permits each stage to be integrated over time.

On-site learning opportunities make it possible for participants to immediately apply what they're learning with a group of familiar children.

On-site learning opportunities make it possible for participants to immediately apply what they're learning with a group of familiar children. The focus of training is to get application of the principles on a daily basis. Off-site classes are frequently too abstract to permit the transfer. Somehow, the distance from the reality of the children and the families served permits a level of abstraction that is difficult to bridge. On-site training permits transfer directly to daily practice and elicits questions drawn from experience.

Good staff development is conducted in a safe atmosphere. All questions are accepted as legitimate; trial and error are encouraged. Jokes about doing better next time or trying harder to get it are out of place. Regimental toughening up exercises may work well in the Marine Corps, but early childhood educators work with children, and blocks to success should be removed for both. Safe, friendly environments are just as essential for effective staff development as they are for young children's healthy development.

Excellent adult educational opportunities require a less-is-more approach. Concepts are repeated from different points of view and in a number of settings so adults gradually see the application with children. As training proceeds, the experiences—of teaching to apply what is being learned, and of observing others teach—gradually are integrated into a useful body of knowledge linked to skills. Lectures and reading appear to be the least useful means to alter classroom practices.

Several outcomes seem to occur again and again as a result of this type of staff development. Most important is the sense of empowerment that adults feel when they realize that children are participants in the learning process and not just receivers of knowledge or protagonists in a forced and uncomfortable setting. Next, adults seem amazed as they learn to share control with children. They learn that adults have a choice in the classroom. They know what to do, how to understand child behavior, and how to capitalize on this positive relationship. With choice, adults can learn and grow to match the freedom and responsibility they share with children.

References

Deming, W.E. (1986). *Out of the crisis*. Cambridge, MA: Cambridge University Press.

Epstein, A.S. (1993). *Training for quality: Improving early childhood programs through systematic in-service training*. Ypsilanti, MI: High/Scope Press.

Preparing Caregivers for Quality Infant and Toddler Child Care

J. Ronald Lally, Carol Lou Young-Holt, and Peter Mangione

We believe there are fundamental philosophical principles that need to be embodied within any comprehensive professional development program related to the group care of infants and toddlers. First, we describe these premises. Then we describe the salient features of a comprehensive training system, *The Program for Infant/Toddler Caregivers*, which is based on these principles.

Principles of quality care for infants and toddlers

According to the 1990 National Child Care Survey (Hofferth, Brayfield, Deich, & Holcomb, 1991), 23% of children younger than age 1, 33% of 1-year-olds, 38% of 2-year-olds, and 50% of 3-year-olds are cared for outside their home in regulated and unregulated family child care and in infant/toddler centers. Thus, many young children spend large amounts of time as part of a group and much of their behavior and feelings are influenced by that group experience.

Group care is a critical variable in the emotional and intellectual development of any child cared for outside the home. As trainers of those who care for these children we need to consider seriously the challenge that faces us. The *Program for Infant/Toddler Caregivers* recommends child care strategies and structures that are based on sound developmental research and theory. Group care influences the foundations for intellectual and emotional development of infants and toddlers.

Five key components of early group experience that affect development are listed here with critical questions and issues for consideration:

(1) Group size and quality of the environment

What is the size of the group and how is the environment structured?

Is it easy or difficult for the child to form intimate relationships with caregivers and children because of the size of the group?

Is the environment safe and interesting or does it lead to conflicts in which biting, toy pulling, dazed wandering, and similar behaviors occur?

(2) Primary caregiving assignments

Are there primary care assignments? Without primary caregivers, infants often have no one person with whom they feel close during long portions of the child care day. In other words, they are not intimately connected with anyone special in the care setting.

(3) Continuity of care

Is there continuity of care? Having one caregiver over an extended period of time rather than switching every six to nine months or so is important to a child's sense of security and connection. Without continuity of care, infants have to establish new primary relationships repeatedly.

(4) Cultural and familial continuity

Is there cultural continuity between home and child care? If there is no one who speaks the child's home language, or validates the childrearing values and beliefs of the family, the early development of identity is threatened.

(5) Meeting the needs of the individual within the group context

How are individual differences handled in the group? What is the temperamental mix of the group of children and caregivers? How does a particular infant's temperament relate to the temperamental traits of the other children in the group? For example, is the child intimidated, ignored, frustrated, or left with the feeling of no boundaries because of unique charac-

Many young children spend large amounts of time as part of a group and much of their behavior and feelings are influenced by that group experience.

A close relationship between caregiver and child and conditions that foster the development of the child's sense of security, confidence, and identity are essential to quality care.

teristics of temperament different from others in the group? Are group needs considered over the needs of each individual child within the group?

These issues are examined in depth in *The Program for Infant/Toddler Caregivers*. The Program's philosophical foundation, grounded in developmental knowledge, determines best practices in group programs for infants and toddlers. We now turn to a description of the training and delivery system.

A comprehensive, multimedia training system

The Child Development Division of the California Department of Education initiated the development of a comprehensive training system for both center- and home-based providers of group care to infants and toddlers in 1986. J. Ronald Lally, director of The Center for Child and Family Studies at Far West Laboratory, developed this system. Funding to support this project came from a number of major private foundations including the Carnegie Corporation and Ford and Harris Foundations. This summary of the development and content of the program, along with training and dissemination initiatives, draws heavily upon Mangione's description (1990).

Program development

The centerpiece of *The Program for Infant/Toddler Caregivers* is a series of broadcast-quality training videos, produced in three languages (English, Spanish, and Chinese), and supplemented and supported by various written materials, including a series of guides on infant and toddler caregiving and group leader manuals.

Content. *The Program for Infant/Toddler Caregivers* is a professional development system which comprehensively covers early development and caregiving practices. It recommends program management strategies and policies which enable optimal care of infants and toddlers in group care, and addresses adult learning issues. The major content areas and core curriculum materials (video and print) are divided into modules on Social Emotional Growth and Socialization; Group Care; Learning and Development; and Culture, Family, and Providers. Leadership development includes seminars and other instructional exchanges with national experts and program staff. Activities for each module focus on adult learning and teaching strategies.

Rationale for using video. The importance of becoming a sensitive observer is seen as an essential part of learning about how to care for infants and toddlers appropriately and effectively. The series of videotapes support development of observational skills. Videotaped material can be highlighted with visual effects and narration to draw viewer's attention to subtleties of infant behavior, and to help caregivers become more sensitive observers. In addition to the importance of observation as a teaching-learning strategy, the accessibility of staff development through broadcast video and its transportability to large numbers of group leaders were important considerations.

Materials and needs assessment. A review of other media training materials (Honig & Wittmer, 1988) revealed that topics such as designing environments for groups of infants, individual variation within a group, and dealing with parental concerns and needs received little treatment.

Information was then gathered from caregivers in center-based programs and family child care to identify their needs, preferences for alternative approaches to learning, and ideas about different contexts for learning. The information gained from 405 child care providers in California, and from national and state advisory panels, was used to establish the priorities for development of videos, print materials, and the system's group leader approach.

Advisory panels. A statement of guidelines for quality care established the project's foundation (California Department of Education, 1988b). The California Child Development Division and national and state experts, researchers, and practitioners contributed to creation of the document, which became the basis for the state's infant and toddler programs and a program quality review instrument.

Guidelines for high quality care. The philosophical core guiding the creation of the program's video and print materials, as well as the content and teaching-learning strategies used in group sessions, centers around infants' need for warm, supportive relationships with caregivers. A close relationship between caregiver and child and conditions that foster the development of the child's sense of security, confidence, and identity are essential to quality care. Moreover, quality care springs from a compassionate understanding of development and respect for each child as an individual with personal needs and inclinations.

The formative role of family history and culture in the lives of infants and toddlers and their families is also considered essential. Establishing a partnership with families based on sensitivity and respect is a vital part of caring for young children.

If there is no one who speaks the child's home language, or validates the childrearing values and beliefs of the family, the early development of identity is threatened.

In 1990, Far West Laboratory, in collaboration with the Child Development Division of the California Department of Education, began a four-part Trainer Intensive series to prepare those providing professional development services to infant/toddler caregivers, family home providers, early intervention program staff members, and teen parents. Trainer Institutes are held four times annually for four days.

The series provides an opportunity for leaders to participate in a comprehensive review and study of the program's philosophy and curriculum. Members of *The Program for Infant/Toddler Caregivers* development staff at Far West Laboratory and key advisors from the Child Development Division lead the groups. Participants include community college and university faculty; program directors, educational coordinators, and site supervisors from state, federal, military, and corporate-funded infant/toddler programs; early intervention, school-age parenting/infant development (SAPID), and teen parent and regional occupational programs (ROP); R &

Dissemination of the staff development program

R agencies, county offices of education; Parent & Child Centers (PCC); Comprehensive Child Development Programs (CCDP); and independent trainers and consultants.

Each of California's resource and referral (R & R) agencies received complimentary copies of all print and video materials for their libraries. Program videos are regularly shown on PBS within California and increasingly in other parts of the nation as well. Pennsylvania set up resource libraries that include sets of the program materials, and uses the *Visions* document and the *Program Quality Review* (PQR) (California State Depart-

Quality care springs from a compassionate understanding of development and respect for each child as an individual with personal needs and inclinations.

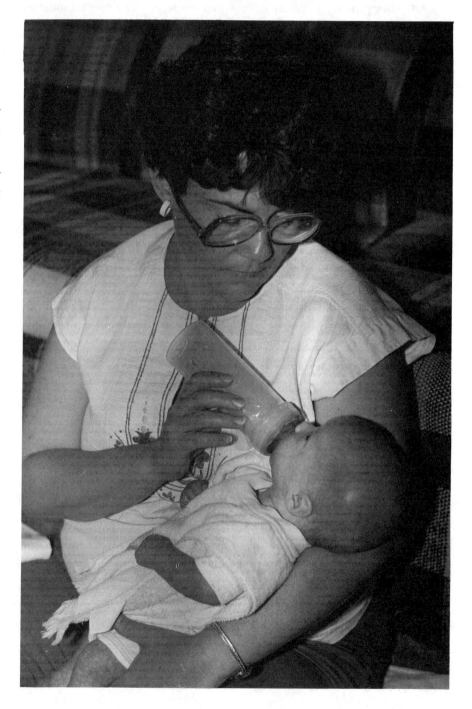

Establishing a partnership with families based on sensitivity and respect is a vital part of caring for young children.

ment of Education, 1988a) instrument in quality improvement work with infant/toddler programs throughout the state.

The Program for Infant/Toddler Caregivers consists of a series of broadcast-quality videos, trainers' manuals, curriculum guides written by nationally recognized experts, and other related materials. Titles include among others, *Flexible, Fearful, or Feisty: The Different Temperaments of Infants and Toddlers; Getting in Tune: Creating Nurturing Relationships with Infants and Toddlers; Together in Care: Meeting the Intimacy Needs of Infants and Toddlers;* and *The Ages of Infancy: Caring for Young, Mobile, and Older Infants.* For information about how to order video and print materials, call the California Department of Education, Child Development Division, 916-322-6233.

Training Intensives are offered to program managers and other professionals responsible for training caregivers in four areas: social/emotional developmental and socialization; group care; learning and development, and culture, family, and providers. For information on the training intensives, contact: Terry DeMartini, Center for Child and Family Studies, Far West Laboratory, 180 Harbor Drive, Suite 112, Sausalito, CA 94965, 415-331-5277, FAX 415-331-0301.

Videos and training institutes

References

California State Department of Education. (1988a). *Infant/Toddler Program Quality Review Instrument.* Sacramento, CA: Author.

California State Department of Education. (1988b). *Visions for infant/toddler care: Guidelines for professional caregiving.* Sacramento, CA: Author.

Hofferth, S.L., Brayfield, A., Deich, S., & Holcomb, P. (1991). *The national child care survey 1990.* Washington, DC: The Urban Institute.

Honig, A.S., & Wittmer, D.S. (1988). *Infant/toddler caregiving: An annotated guide to media training materials.* Sacramento, CA: California State Department of Education.

Mangione, P. (1990). A comprehensive approach to using video for training infant and toddler caregivers. *Infants and Young Children, 3*(1), 61–68.

The Family-to-Family Project: Developing Family Child Care Providers

Nancy Cohen and Kathy Modigliani

The Family-to-Family initiative funded by the Dayton Hudson Foundation is designed to improve the quality of family child care by providing staff development opportunities, accreditation, and parent education to providers. The Project, implemented in 32 sites around the country, offers comprehensive learning opportunities. An average of 90 providers are served at single-site projects each year; multi-site projects serve an average of 210 providers annually.

Staff development arrangements

Components of staff development opportunities vary at Family-to-Family sites, and include courses, self-study, home visits, and mentor programs. Each site is required to offer a course of at least 15 hours to address business start-up and management; local regulations; health, safety, and nutrition; child development and age-appropriate activities; discipline; children with special needs; parent-provider relationships; professional development and community resources; cultural and ethnic issues; and personal and family development.

Most Project coordinators and group leaders customize one or more family child care curricula to their own teaching styles and their perceptions of what providers need (see Modigliani, 1991).

The Family-to-Family Project demonstrates that providers are willing and able to pay for their learning opportunities. Sites charge a wide range of user fees, from no cost to $50 for a 36-hour course (at least half of the providers qualify for scholarships). Staff members at many sites initially thought providers would value their experiences more by paying. Early research indicates that the amount charged is not correlated with success in meeting learning goals.

These approaches were used by various sites to develop fee structures for adult education:

- Charge most of the cost and give scholarships to lower-income providers.
- Charge a separate fee for each level.
- Charge providers at the beginning, lend them manuals, and then at the end of the course sell manuals to providers who want them.
- Increase the price over three years as the project becomes better known and popular.
- Where regulation is voluntary, charge unregulated providers more than the regulated providers. This promotes regulation.

Several important lessons were learned by the Family-to-Family Project about effective professional development of family child care providers.

Among the most important in terms of professionalization of the field are instructor characteristics, techniques that maximize learning, and the impact of training on quality of care.

Skillful trainers can adapt mediocre curricula. Even the best curricula, however, cannot compensate for unskilled group leaders. Experiences at the Family-to-Family sites suggest that effective instructors have a combination of characteristics:

- **Knowledge of and respect for family child care. Several years experience as a successful family child care provider.** Providers seem to prefer and learn more from instructors who are currently or have been providers. They should also be familiar with other provider homes and have pursued more formal education themselves. Instructors without

Characteristics of effective instructors

Providers seem to prefer and learn more from instructors who are currently or have been providers.

Providers who learn more are likely to stay in the field longer because they feel more professional, are more effective in their work, and find it easier.

Mentor and partner programs help providers learn, complete the course, and increase their self-esteem.

experience as providers can be successful if they take the time to learn about family child care by visiting provider homes and meeting with groups of providers to learn about their day-to-day joys, stresses, and needs. It is particularly important for instructors without experience as providers to encourage learning among those in the group.

- **Knowledge of child development and early childhood education.** A comprehensive understanding of these fields is required to answer providers' questions and facilitate discussion. When provider instructors feel weak in these areas, experts are invited to lead the sessions.

- **Knowledge of how adults learn.** Successful instructors understand principles of adult education. They offer practical information that providers can implement immediately. Providers choose what they want to learn based on their interests. Providers are encouraged to learn from each other's experiences (Modigliani, 1991). Long lectures are rare; classes are often interactive.

- **Ability to form personal relationships with providers.** Successful instructors are often warm people who grow to know each student. Providers who have personal relationships with instructors seem to be better able to question their practices and change their behavior. Also, close relationships with instructors encourage providers to complete the curriculum and take additional courses. A major benefit of home visits is the chance for instructors and providers to get to know each other better.

- **Experience in giving presentations and co-teaching.** In most cases, at the beginning of the Family-to-Family Projects, staff members do not know many providers. One strategy used to identify provider instructors is to ask providers who graduate from the first class to give presentations on specific topics during the next class. This technique has the added benefit of improving the provider's presentation skills and varying the mode of instruction for students, who enjoy being taught by peers. Co-teaching is most successful when experienced instructors involve providers in all aspects of planning and delivery of training.

Techniques that maximize learning

A variety of teaching strategies are used with adult learners in the Family-to-Family Project.

- Mentor and partner programs help providers learn, complete the course, and increase their self-esteem. These programs give providers personal attention and individual help, validate that a peer is able to help them, and act as a motivator to complete the course.

- Self-study is a stepping stone to classroom-based experiences for some providers.

- Programs for non-English-speaking providers are needed at most sites. The three sites that offer training to non-English-speaking providers experience the most success by offering separate classes conducted in the providers' languages.

- Providers may be more motivated when they have clear goals such as completion activities, NAFCC accreditation, or CDA credentialing.
- Providers seem to enjoy implementing what they learn. However, if providers are not required to use their new knowledge, they may not try or are likely to find the experience less rewarding.
- Use of videotapes during home visits to demonstrate activities and techniques is seen as informative and motivating.
- Comprehensive systems for family child care providers' development offer basic preparation and then more advanced courses. After providers finish one level, most are interested in more advanced courses.

Providers report that learning opportunities increase their professionalism and self-esteem, and improve the care they offer.

- **Learning seems to increase providers' sense of professionalism.** Prepared providers say they no longer see their work with young children as just "babysitting," but as a skill that requires development. Learning establishes more commitment to deliver high-quality child care.
- **Provider development seems to increase self-esteem.** Deciding to take and complete courses are major accomplishments for many providers. In some cases, this is their first positive experience with formal education. Many providers also mention that these experiences help them recognize the things they do well. Some providers report staying in the field longer as a result of the program.
- **Courses for providers seem to improve their health and safety practices, business practices, and knowledge of how children learn.**

Impact of provider development on service quality

The success of the Family-to-Family Project documents that many family child care providers are willing to take courses that are 15 hours or longer. Most providers who start the courses complete them; the average retention rate is 85 to 95%. Courses, more than isolated workshops, may promote retention because

- Providers have time to learn techniques that make their jobs easier and more rewarding. They learn a new technique in class, practice it at home, discuss it at the next class, and try it again. Providers who learn more are likely to stay in the field longer because they feel more professional, are more effective in their work, and find it easier.
- Courses have the unintended, but fortunate, effect of starting or building provider associations. Belonging to associations or keeping in touch with other providers seems to help providers stay in business.
- Courses create new roles for providers as teachers, presenters, and mentors. Many providers who fill these roles, while continuing to care for children, find the new roles make them more enthusiastic about direct care and appreciative of career development opportunities.

In many communities, the only courses available before the Family-to-Family Project were targeted to center-based caregivers. Providers prefer

Lessons for the field

family provider-focused courses because

- They address the unique needs of family child care such as working with children of different ages, preparing meals for children while caring for them, and dealing directly with parents.
- Providers are able to socialize as well as be role models for each other.
- The examples used to illustrate techniques are from family child care and are easily transferable; center-based examples are often difficult to transfer into practice for family child care.
- Instructors and other students do not look down on family child care as "babysitters" as is sometimes the case in courses with center-based providers.

The funding organization's investment has enabled the 26 Family-to-Family sites to experiment with some of the most comprehensive training for family child care providers available in the United States. The lessons emerging from these projects—about what works and what does not—have moved the field ahead significantly in its ability to promote the professional development of family child care providers.

Reference   Modigliani, K. (1991). *Training programs for family child care providers: An analysis of ten curricula.* Boston: Wheelock College Family Child Care Project. (ERIC Document Reproduction Service No. ED 354 104)

Effective Practices in Staff Development: Head Start Experiences

Barbara L. Wolfe

Research related to changes in teaching practices as a result of staff development experiences is sparse. "Although a majority of investigations in teacher training measure the acquisition of knowledge and skill, only a few of the studies examine whether those skills are integrated and maintained in the teacher's active teaching repertoire" (Joyce & Showers, 1980, p. 381). Bennett's survey of the literature uncovered just 20 studies that reported on transfer of learning (1987).

Staff development is of particular importance to Head Start. It is the largest early childhood program in the nation, employing 109,345 paid staff in 1992 (U.S. Department of Health and Human Services, 1993). A majority of the program's teachers enter the field without a baccalaureate degree in early childhood education, so orientation and on-the-job learning are emphasized. Head Start was instrumental in instituting the Child Development Associate (CDA) Credential, and as of September 30, 1994, requires that at least one teacher in each classroom hold a CDA Credential or other appropriate qualification. The program provides a formal national training and technical assistance network and allocates funds earmarked for staff development to each program. With this history and commitment to staff development, Head Start offers fertile territory for research on the issue.

An exploratory research project conducted by the author in 1990 was designed to identify what practices Head Start staff believe can facilitate the transfer of learning experiences to work with groups of young children (Wolfe, 1990). Survey results are briefly reviewed here along with their implications for early childhood professional development.

A survey, developed in conjunction with Head Start staff and professional development experts, was distributed to 128 Head Start staff members from 32 randomly selected grantees (13 in Michigan, 11 in Wisconsin, and 8 in Minnesota). The sample of programs included 13 small grantees (fewer than 200 children), 14 medium-sized grantees (200 to 499 children), and 5 large grantees (more than 500 children).

Responses were received from 122 people (96%). Their experience in Head Start ranged from 1 to 24 years; the average was 10. Seventy-four participants had earned at least a college degree, 48 had less than a college degree. Of the non-degreed respondents, 31 had a CDA Credential. Teachers accounted for 65 of the responses; 57 were received from disabilities and/or education coordinators.

Training strategy preferences. Given a list of 22 training strategies

Staff development is of particular importance to Head Start.

Survey responses and results

Survey results confirm that effective adult education is complex and requires more than isolated one-shot workshops.

from which to choose, respondents reported experience most often (in order) with: lecture, small group discussion, handouts, videos/movies, games/ simulations. The strategies experienced least often were (in descending order): follow-up meetings, follow-up letters, back-home plans, follow-up phone calls, and micro-teaching (videotaping of sample lessons).

When asked which four training strategies they would recommend be included in any in-service they attend, participants suggested: small group discussion (54%), demonstration/modeling (47%), handouts (38%), lecture (37%), observing actual practice (34%), games/simulations (28%), role play (24%), video/movies (20%). The least recommended instructional strategies were (in descending order): follow-up letters, worksheets, instrumented learning (i.e., tests, questionnaires, surveys), assignments, and follow-up phone calls.

When asked to rate the 22 training strategies according to how much change they promote on the job, the highest-ranking strategies were: observing actual practice, follow-up job assistance, small group discussion, handouts, demonstration/modeling, and follow-up meetings. Respondents who experienced follow-up job assistance (41) or follow-up meetings (60) rated the strategies highly. Strategies indicated as least likely to promote transfer were: worksheets, follow-up letters, resources, panel discussion, assignments, and instrumented learning.

Instructor characteristics. Given a list of 16 instructor characteristics and asked to select the five most important, participants picked the following traits: well-prepared (76%); knowledgeable about the subject (72%), provides opportunities for hands-on experiences and interaction among participants (51%), enthusiastic (48%), uses a variety of training techniques (41%).

Contextual variables. Participants were given a list of 27 contextual variables and asked to rate each according to how important it was in helping them make changes as a result of the in-service experience. The following were the highest-rated contextual variables, and all were significantly related to the highest rating of "very important": the trainer was effective, the topic met a need I had at the time, the in-service content was practical, the in-service gave me genuine opportunity for professional growth, I enjoyed the in-service, the staff members in my program had a good working relationship.

The lowest-rated contextual variables, in descending order, were significantly related to the lowest rating category, "not important at all": administrators told us we had to make the changes presented, the content was addressed over several days, I was involved in planning the in-service, I was specially selected to take part in the in-service, the in-service was for credit.

Participants were then asked to list the three most important factors that assist them to transfer learning to the job. The most frequently mentioned factors were: handouts/materials provided for later reference, content meets a need/is relevant, support of staff and/or administrators following training, content is practical, effective trainer, opportunities to observe, opportunities to practice.

Survey results confirm that effective adult education is complex and requires more than isolated one-shot workshops. In-service efforts that enable participants to make changes must be relevant to the participants' needs, conducted by effective instructors, supported by agency administrators and co-workers, include opportunities to observe and practice what is presented, and accompanied by follow-up efforts which engage participants.

Results of this survey indicate that professional development opportunities can be augmented in these ways.

Implications for staff development

Questions about staff development

1. What can supervisors do to help ensure learning transfer when staff attend a conference or workshop?

Ask staff to prepare an action plan before they go. What do they hope to gain from the experience? What questions do they have on the topic? What are they doing to prepare to learn?

Sit down with staff immediately after they return and ask: Where do you go from here with your action plan? What did you learn? What ideas can you implement first? By when? How can I help you?

Two weeks to one month later, conduct another meeting to report on progress and brainstorm solutions to any implementation challenges.

2. In planning staff development sessions, what strategies help participants transfer learning?

To facilitate the use of new skills, incorporate these techniques: presentation of information; demonstration (games, role plays, videotape of good practices); feedback (after implementing ideas, discuss what went well and identify areas for improvement); small-group discussion (talk about new strategies and share implementation ideas); action planning (ask participants to outline what they'll do differently as the result of the workshop).

3. How can lectures be made more interesting?

Use visual aids that are visible and interesting (charts, overheads, videos, slides, teaching materials).

Ask questions frequently. Encourage participants to share opinions, examples, and to synthesize what they've learned.

Use lots of examples and anecdotes to illustrate points.

Guide note taking by giving an outline of the presentation.

Encourage discussion. Divide into small groups or pairs and give each a problem, question, or case study to address.

Use a game format to review material.

4. What are effective ways to conduct needs assessments?

Use a checklist of potential topics that staff prioritize according to their needs.

Use a competency inventory or job description for staff to rate themselves on the skills needed to do their jobs. The same tool can be used to rate staff members and compare perceptions. The skills rated lowest are the basis for planning staff development.

5. What are effective strategies to motivate staff during in-service training?

Four motivational factors are: success + volition (choice) + value + enjoyment. If these can be incorporated in training, staff will probably be motivated. Instructors should think about ways to help staff feel successful, provide choices, show them the value of the experience, and help them have a good time.

Instructors should think about ways to help staff feel successful, provide choices, show them the value of the experience, and help them have a good time.

- Conduct needs assessments that genuinely reflect the concerns and growth needs of participants—not of administrators. Needs assessment should be ongoing and designed to reflect changing training needs, not a yearly exercise to complete training plans.

- Ensure that administrators understand and endorse what is being presented and that they have a commitment to support change.

- Move beyond standard lecture formats to include time within the in-service for observation and practice opportunities which closely simulate the work setting. More intensive workshops are essential for transfer of learning.

- Include discussion among participants to decide what to do and share ideas about how to do it.

- Highlight important points on handouts.

- Be well prepared, be knowledgeable about the subject, and show enthusiasm for the topic.

- Include follow-up as an integral part of the in-service delivery system: meetings, on-site visitations, or sessions.

References

Joyce, B., & Showers, B. (1980). Improving inservice training: The messages of research. *Educational Leadership, 37,* 379–385.

Showers, B., Joyce, B., & Bennett, B. (1987). Synthesis of research on staff development: A framework for future study and a state of the art analysis. *Educational Leadership, 45*(3), 77–87.

U.S. Department of Health and Human Services. (1993). Project Head Start Statistical Fact Sheet. Washington, DC: U.S. Government Printing Office.

Wolfe, B. (1990). *Effective practices in inservice education: An exploratory study of the perceptions of Head Start participants.* Unpublished doctoral dissertation, University of Wisconsin, Madison.

Professional Development for Leaders: Lessons from Head Start

Paula Jorde Bloom

Directors have a powerful influence on the climate of their programs—both as a work place for the staff and as an educational and nurturing environment for young children. Therefore, the director's skills and knowledge have a profound impact on the quality of services. Despite considerable evidence about the importance of specialized job preparation, few directors of early childhood programs have formal education about the principles of organizational theory, leadership styles, program administration, staff development, community and board relations, or group dynamics. Most directors are promoted to their positions because of exemplary performance as teachers or because of longevity at their agency, not because they have expertise in program leadership.

Most directors are promoted to their positions because of exemplary performance as teachers, not because they have expertise in program leadership.

In response to this situation, National-Louis University (NLU) launched the Early Childhood Leadership and Advocacy Program. This field-based master's degree program is designed to accommodate the needs of early childhood educators who want to expand their repertoire of administrative and leadership skills without interrupting their careers. Since 1984, approximately 350 students have graduated from this program.

A perennial problem in directing this graduate program has been how to find creative solutions to the financial dilemma that confronts many early childhood educators—they are eager to pursue advanced course work, but cannot afford the tuition and fees. In 1989, NLU received a grant from the U.S. Department of Health and Human Services to train Head Start directors. The 31 candidates selected to participate were chosen because of their leadership potential for becoming mentor/trainers of Head Start supervisors. Two cohorts of participants from Head Start programs throughout the Chicago metropolitan area began the leadership program in September 1989 and culminated their studies in December 1990. This professional development model and its outcomes have important implications for the field.

The content of the Early Childhood Leadership and Advocacy Program covers all components of the director's role (see Bloom, Sheerer, Richard, & Britz, 1991). The program usually takes 20 months; the contract for the Head Start group necessitated a 16-month cycle. Participants meet for 77 four-hour sessions. In addition, individual conferences are held as necessary. Participants receive 32 semester hours of graduate credit leading to a master's degree in Early Childhood Leadership and Advocacy.

This leadership program is unique in content and implementation. Many adult learners are frustrated by the inevitable gap between the theoretical

The professional development model

This model rests on the assumption that immediate application from new learning to real-life situations reinforces what is learned.

ideas encountered in their studies and their ability to apply these ideas in their work. This model rests on the assumption that immediate application from new learning to real-life situations reinforces what is learned. It emphasizes pragmatic links between theory, research, and practice in three important ways:

- The curriculum is problem-centered and site-specific. The examples relate to real, daily issues and concerns.
- Participants are actively involved in applied research. They each identify an issue relevant to their professional needs and design a research study around that issue. In the process, they become not only consumers of research who study and apply the work of others, but also researchers themselves, creating knowledge and learning to think critically about educational ideas and practices.
- Finally, for the two Head Start groups that went through the program, instructors visited each participant at her or his work site. Instructors assessed participants' learning needs and monitored their progress during the course of the project.

Effectiveness of the model

There are many ways to assess the effectiveness of a professional development model—feedback from the participants regarding changes in their knowledge and skills; feedback from the supervisors and colleagues attesting to changes in behavior or attitudes; and independent observations by an outside party looking at changes in actual on-the-job behavior. Multiple perspectives increase the reliability and validity of results by decreasing the possibility of bias.

All these approaches were incorporated in evaluating the Head Start Leadership Training Program. Out of the 31 Head Start participants, 22 had direct responsibility for the quality of teaching practices in their centers (9 directors and 13 head teachers). These 22 individuals were the target group for evaluation. To provide comparison data, a sample of 22 Head Start teachers and directors who did not participate in the program was recruited. A t-test was conducted on each background variable to discern if the groups were evenly matched prior to training; no statistically significant differences surfaced.

Level of perceived competence. The participants' level of perceived competence was measured by the Training Needs Assessment Survey (TNAS), which assesses the level of perceived competence in 28 knowledge and skill areas related to early childhood program leadership. These 28 areas cluster in five task performance areas: personal and professional self-knowledge; child development and early childhood programming; organizational theory, leadership, and program administration; parent relations, community relations, public policy, and advocacy; and research and technology.

On a 5-point scale, respondents were asked to indicate their level of knowledge or skill in each of the 28 areas (from 1 = no knowledge in this area to 5 = extremely knowledgeable). The total possible range of scores was 28 to 140. The TNAS was administered before the program sequence began to help assess each participant's needs and to provide baseline data on participants' level of perceived competence. It was administered again at the end of the 16-month cycle to document any changes in perceived level of competence in the 28 knowledge and skill areas. A comparison of pretest and posttest data revealed a strong, statistically significant increase in participants' levels of perceived competence in all five clusters.

When program participants were asked to reflect on how they had grown professionally in the program, most responses related to a gain in self-confidence, which in turn seemed to translate into a stronger professional conviction and a resurgence of energy and enthusiasm relative to early childhood education.

- *I stretched this year. I stepped out with both feet and didn't fall. In fact, I flew! I thank you all for touching my life so inspirationally, so positively.*
- *Thank you, you saved my life! I was slowly dying professionally—I was in a rut. You have opened my eyes, enhanced my self-esteem, and motivated me to get involved in early childhood issues. I've always liked young children, but I had begun to get stale. I've developed pride in my career choice and feel competent. My life has been enriched and I am grateful!*

Quality of teaching practices. A modified version of the Early Childhood Classroom Observation Scale developed for NAEYC accreditation was used to assess the quality of teaching practices in four areas: interactions among staff and children; curriculum; health, safety, and nutrition; and the physical environment. Each criterion was rated on a scale of 1 (not met) to 4 (fully met). The total classroom quality score could range from 58 to 232. An early childhood specialist who is on the faculty of NLU served as the classroom observer for both the pretest and posttest observations to ensure reliability.

A series of t-tests was conducted to discern if the two groups were evenly matched at the beginning of the training period. None of the four subscales on the pretest revealed statistically significant differences between the two groups. On the posttest scores, the mean overall quality score for the target group was 207.26 (an increase of 33 points). The mean posttest score for the comparison group was 169.75 (a decrease of 3 points).

Another series of t-tests was conducted to discern if there were statistically significant differences in the mean change scores that might be attributable to the program experience. On all four subscales and on the overall classroom quality scores, the participants consistently had higher, significantly different, scores on posttest observations.

Quality of work life/organizational climate. The Early Childhood Work Environment Survey (ECWES) was used to assess the quality of work life for staff employed at the centers of the directors in the leadership group. The ECWES measures ten dimensions of organizational climate (collegiality, opportunities for professional growth, supervisor support, clarity, reward

Program participants reported a gain in self-confidence, which in turn seemed to translate into a stronger professional conviction and a resurgence of energy and enthusiasm.

Staff development experiences can have a direct effect on participants' perceived level of competence, the quality of their teaching practices, and the organizational climate of their centers.

system, decision-making structure, goal consensus, task orientation, physical environment, and innovativeness). Organizational climate is defined as the collective perceptions of staff regarding these ten dimensions. A score of 0 to 10 is generated for each dimension of organizational climate by averaging employee responses to ten items for each dimension.

The ECWES also measures the staff's level of decision-making influence and their level of desired decision-making influence (each subscale ranges from 0 to 10). Finally, the ECWES measures staff's perceptions of how their current work environment compares with their ideal (scores range from 10 to 50). The ECWES was administered prior to the start and at the culmination of the program. On nine of the ten dimensions, the staff employed at the participating Head Start centers expressed more positive attitudes about the climate of their programs. In three of the ten dimensions (opportunities for professional growth, clarity, and degree of innovativeness) the differences in mean scores reached statistical significance.

Staff expressed stronger levels of commitment to their centers at the end of the program ($t = 2.53$, $p < .01$). Another interesting result surfaced in the area of staff's perceptions of their current decision-making influence. Statistically significant differences between the pretest and the posttest administration of the ECWES may be attributable to the professional development experience. The strongest differences in staff's perceptions, however, occurred in the "congruence with ideal" subscale. The pretest mean score on this subscale was 36.08; the posttest score was 42.53 ($t = 4.37$, $p < .0001$).

Implications for the field

The evaluation of this leadership training program provides compelling evidence that staff development experiences can have a direct effect on participants' perceived level of competence, the quality of their teaching practices, and the organizational climate of their centers. Two important themes emerge that warrant attention: the potency of the learning experiences as they relate to participants' increased feelings of self-efficacy and participants' ability to effect positive changes in their programs.

With respect to self-confidence and self-efficacy, participants reported significantly higher levels of perceived competence in 28 knowledge and skill areas. These data were supported by personal reflections of how individuals grew and changed through this educational experience. The program format, based on an adult development model, encouraged the sharing of experiential knowledge. It also emphasized the written and verbal expression of ideas. As students received positive feedback as well as constructive criticism from instructors who validated their efforts and ideas, they were willing to take more risks in articulating a point of view and even modifying their position on issues.

The overriding goal of the leadership experience was to empower participants to effect change in their Head Start programs. The observations of classroom quality conducted as part of the evaluation confirms that it may well have had a pronounced impact on the quality of teaching practices in the classroom. A significant improvement—in the interactions between adults and children; the classroom curriculum; the arrangement and use of the physical environment; and health, safety, and nutritional practices—was noted at the end of the 16-month period. These same changes were not detected in the comparison group.

Feedback from the participants' colleagues and their supervisors also provides evidence regarding the strength and direction of these changes. It appears that improving participants' repertoires of administrative and organizational skills had a direct impact on many organizational practices. Previous research in this area would lead one to be cautious in expecting changes in staff attitudes about organizational climate in such a short time, but the results of the data analysis revealed a surprising increase in positive perceptions. Significant changes—in employees' perceptions of organizational climate with respect to the clarity of program policies and procedures, the degree of program innovativeness, and opportunities for professional growth—were seen in the posttest administration of the ECWES. In addition, a significant increase in level of employee commitment to their centers and more favorable attitudes about their perceived level of decision-making influence were noted.

Conducting action research changes the early childhood profession from the inside out and from the bottom up, through changes in early childhood educators themselves.

The rich anecdotal evidence from participants at the culmination of the leadership program provides first-hand accounts of how conducting action research changes the early childhood profession from the inside out and from the bottom up, through changes in early childhood educators themselves. It appears that the research component of this model has the potential to play a significant role in improving the quality of services provided to children and their families. By becoming researchers, teachers take control over their classrooms and professional lives in ways that confound the traditional definition of teacher and offer proof that education can reform itself from within.

The principal barrier in carrying out this professional development effort was time. The original proposal called for a 20-month program. The funding cycle for the grant necessitated that it be condensed to 16 months. Before the project was launched, it was feared that the pace of the program might be too rigorous. The dedication and commitment of the individuals who took part was outstanding, but program staff have concerns about the levels of stress participants may have experienced due to the accelerated pace. It is recommended that future endeavors to replicate this model be structured to ensure a full 20 to 22 months.

Conclusions

Encouraging child care directors to pursue advanced study in early childhood leadership can be problematic. Limited financial resources, time constraints, and the lack of external support are but a few of the obstacles directors and teachers experience when considering graduate work. The structure and design of this model helped alleviate some of these problems.

A cost-effective, easily implemented in-service model has broad implications for improving the professional expertise of early childhood program directors while promoting substantive change and improvement in the quality of care for young children.

Many individuals feel insecure about attending university courses after having been out of school for some time. The small-group format of this model provides the collegial support that many mid-career teachers and directors need to reduce anxiety about reentry into a degree program. Moreover, knowing that the degree can be completed in less than two years provides additional incentive to the potentially reluctant, full-time professional. Perhaps the most important incentive, however, is the fact that participants quickly appreciate the emphasis on linking theory to practice. Individuals realize that what they are doing in the program has direct relevance to their work.

Many aspects of this model of leadership development are unique: The length and sequence of the program, the multi-disciplinary content of the curriculum, the cluster format, the site visits by the instructor, the work-related research project, and the link of completion of study to graduate credit. The results suggest this may be a promising model for providing professional growth experiences for early childhood personnel around the country. As a cost-effective, easily implemented in-service model, it has broad implications for improving the professional expertise of early childhood program directors while at the same time promoting substantive change and improvement in the quality of care for young children, their families, and program staff.

References

Bloom, P.J., Sheerer, M., Richard, N., & Britz, J. (1991). *The Head Start Leadership Training Program: Final Report to the Department of Health and Human Services Head Start Division.* Evanston, IL: Early Childhood Professional Development Project, National-Louis University.

Bloom, P.J. (1992, Spring). The child care center director: A critical determinant of program quality. *Educational Horizons, 70,* 138–145.

Additional resources

Bloom, P.J., & Sheerer, M. (1992a). The effect of leadership training on child care program quality. *Early Childhood Research Quarterly, 7*(4), 579–594.

Bloom, P.J., & Sheerer, M. (1992b). Changing organizations by changing individuals: A model of leadership training. *The Urban Review, 24*(4), 263–286.

Professional Development for School-Age Child Care

Susan O'Connor

The School-Age Child Care Project (SACC) was initiated in 1979 to provide research, training, publications, and technical assistance on issues relevant to school-age care. The thrust of the Project's first ten years was on start-up and fundraising. SACC's focus now is quality of care, with a priority to create a system of professional development that reflects the field's needs. There are few formal professional preparation programs distinctly tailored for school-age child care providers, and a patchwork of in-service learning. SACC and the National School-Age Child Care Alliance are exploring options which may lead to creation of such a system.

There are few formal professional preparation programs distinctly tailored for school-age child care providers, and a patchwork of in-service learning.

School-age child care and early childhood education share much common ground:

- Professionals in both fields work with young children. School-age programs increasingly serve 3- and 4-year-olds.
- Much of the same knowledge base is shared. The best school-age child care programs use developmentally appropriate practice as the foundation for their approach.
- Many school-age child care staff have early childhood backgrounds—both Child Development Associate and college credentials. School-age child care is a visible presence at early childhood staff development events and conferences. Many in the field are long-standing members of NAEYC and some programs are NAEYC accredited.
- Both fields share many of the same challenges—a national staffing crisis fueled by low compensation, and turnover rates that continue to create problems for staff continuity and program quality.

School-age child care also differs from early childhood education in many ways:

- Increasingly, older children and youth through age 14 are served in school-age child care programs. A child may enter a program at age four, taking naps and spending endless hours in the dramatic play area. When the child leaves the program at age 14, she or he may be a proficient actor, photographer, swimmer, or builder. Children often develop long-lasting and sophisticated relationships with each other. Many have jobs as caregivers of children, or are only a year away from a regular after-school job. One of the greatest challenges for school-age child care is to provide rich and exciting opportunities for older children.
- School-age child care professionals must be prepared to build prevention programs that create avenues of opportunity for children and youth. Parents are deeply grateful for the refuge that programs provide their children from community violence and poverty.

All too often, the lack of a basic, common body of knowledge for staff means that the majority are inadequately prepared for their role.

· Many school-age program staff do not see themselves as early childhood educators. Their professional identity is more likely to be determined by the place they work or their educational background. They may align more closely with a wide variety of fields that include youth service work, community education, parks and recreation, social work, elementary education, and fine arts.

Drawing people from all these fields can result in a rich tapestry of skills and personal qualities in programs, and there is much to gain from this diversity. But all too often, the lack of a basic, common body of knowledge for staff means that the majority are inadequately prepared for their role. Without any real *system* of preservice or in-service education, the vast potential to enhance children's development through socialization, relaxation, and informal learning is barely tapped. Although some wonderful program directors and committed staff have been able to overcome this

Without any real system of preservice or in-service education, the vast potential to enhance children's development through socialization, relaxation, and informal learning is barely tapped.

hurdle, far too many staff are part of programs that shadow the school day with rigid schedules and few chances for children to make meaningful activity choices. Other programs merely supervise children, in institutional settings, with inadequate supplies and equipment.

There are about 50,000 school-age child care programs in this country (Seppanen, P., Love, J., Kaplan deVries, D., & Bernstein, L., 1993). Children of full-time working parents may actually spend more time in a school-age child care program than they spend at school. Much is at stake for a large number of children, yet almost all school-age child care staff are part-time, and most arrive in programs by default rather than design, on their way to or from another career.

Even the majority of directors are part-time, working an average of 25 hours a week. Most directors have direct responsibilities for children in addition to administrative tasks. Although more than half of directors hold bachelor's or master's degrees, those degrees may have little relevance to the daily requirements of running a program. A person with a bachelor's degree in fine arts or recreation may have to be an expert at learning by the "seat of their pants" to pull off the daily challenges of running a program: balancing the budget and fundraising; recruiting and supervising inexperienced, part-time staff; managing space which may be shared (classroom, gymnasium, or church); board and community relations.

Many directors are isolated, with few in-service opportunities except a day of first-aid training, a workshop on behavior management, or a day at a conference. One leading source of substantial in-service staff development for program directors is the School-Age Child Care Institute, designed in 1986 for Wheelock College by the School-Age Child Care Project. Each year, Institutes are held in various locations around the country, funded by local, state, or federal dollars, or by corporate or foundation support. The SACC Project usually works with a local sponsor to organize the Institute. The local sponsor may be the administrator of the state's Dependent Care Block Grant money, a college that is involved in child care professional development, a child care resource and referral (R & R) agency, or a collaborative sponsorship between a corporation and a public agency.

Institutes serve as many as 40 participants at each site. The local sponsor can choose between a three-day or five-day design. The five-day Institutes provide two graduate credits for participants. Institutes are often held in a retreat-type setting so that participants can fully immerse themselves in the intensive sessions. School-age child care leaders with a broad range of experience and responsibilities are attracted to the Institutes. Sometimes practitioners are joined by staff from licensing agencies or child care R & R agencies.

Leaders work together to tailor the Institute to the participants's needs. A planning questionnaire is sent to each participant to find out what she or he hopes to gain from the experience. Participants choose the topics that are most important to them, allocate the necessary time, and gather addi-

Far too many staff are part of programs that shadow the school day with rigid schedules and few chances for children to make meaningful activity choices.

A person with a bachelor's degree in fine arts or recreation may have to be an expert at learning by the "seat of their pants"

tional resources. They may also ask the sponsor to help them find a local expert to be a guest speaker. For example, in a state that is instituting new regulations, the head of the licensing agency may come to speak. If the majority of participants serve children from low-income families, a panel presentation on sliding fee scales, scholarships, and other subsidies might be in order.

A wide variety of topics are covered by the Institute:

- analysis of elements of high quality school-age child care programs
- review of the developmental needs of children from ages 5 to 13 (and how to provide a curriculum that reflects youths' growing interest in the adult world and their need for independence)
- staff development—recruitment, interviewing, orientation; retention; team building; supervision, development, evaluation
- curriculum development, including a hands-on activities fair
- space design, including an experiential activity with shared space
- improving relationships with children, parents, the "host" of the space, the community, and among staff
- supporting and enhancing diversity—understanding and supporting children and families in crisis, program development for children with special needs, increased attention to multicultural programming, gender equity
- strategic planning
- program assessment and improvement

The key to the Institute's success is its interactive format. Participants' experiences are elicited and plenty of time is scheduled for them to share experiences and frustration, solve problems, and generate new ideas. They leave the Institute invigorated, some with plans to fine-tune their programs, others hoping for a major overhaul. Sometimes they report that it's been difficult to translate new ideas into concrete program improvements. Some get lost again in the day-to-day details of program administration; others can't get staff to accept new ideas.

In an effort to improve links between training and application, and with the support of the AT&T Family Care Development Fund, a new self-assessment instrument, *Assessing School-Age Child Care Quality (ASQ)* was developed (O'Connor, 1991). *ASQ* asks parents, staff, and children to look at what works well and what needs to be improved in their program. Institute participants have a tool to focus on service improvement through program observation, questionnaires, and program-wide dialogue. With this comprehensive model, some programs receive technical assistance from *ASQ* Advisors, local school-age child care experts who are prepared to develop a collaborative relationship with the program and guide the use of *ASQ*. A third college credit is available for participants who work on ASQ and program improvement.

Another SACC training initiative, made possible with the support of an anonymous funder and the Kellogg and Primerica Foundations, involved collaboration with the National Association of Elementary School Principals between 1991 and 1993. Elementary and middle school principals and their community teams took part in a two-day workshop on program start-up and improvement. Teams included school-age child care specialists who provided technical assistance to the group as it initiated or improved school-age programs. In addition, principals participated in a leadership program to enhance their ability to become local resources.

The School-Age Child Care Project and the National School-Age Child Care Alliance are excited about preservice and in-service training opportunities that can lead to a vision of a system for staff development. Both groups will work to

- Identify the parameters of the field, looking at the ages of children, and determining what aspects of early childhood education, youth service work, recreation, social work, and other fields, apply to school-age child care.
- Propose a format and curriculum for preservice professional development based on experiences in the United States and other countries. In Denmark, school-age child care professionals are called *pedagogs* and their professional preparation is tailored to the demands of the field.
- Explore the possibilities of establishing degree programs at two- or four-year institutions of higher education. Links with lab schools, mentoring experiences, and other avenues will be explored to ensure that professionals are truly prepared for their roles.
- Examine in-service learning experiences, and develop a system that enables people to move along a career ladder.

Through all these efforts, the critical contributions and needs of school-age child care staff will be taken into account. Staff diversity is a major goal, just as it is in early childhood education. This agenda is enormous. School-age child care is younger than early childhood education, yet the field is moving quickly. Too much is at stake to linger.

References

O'Connor, S. (1991). *ASQ: Assessing school-age child care quality*. Wellesley, MA: SACC Project Publications.

Seppanen, P., Love, J., Kaplan deVries, D., & Bernstein, L. (1993). *National study of before- and after-school programs*. Portsmouth, NH: RMC Research Corporation.

Constructing Professional Knowledge by Telling Our Stories

Elizabeth Jones

Everyone who comes to the field of early childhood education brings some kind of relevant experiences with young children, experiences which form a foundation on which to construct teaching theory and practice.

The concept of the lattice of early childhood careers and professional development enables the field to move beyond the traditional distinction between preservice and in-service education for teachers of young children. In early childhood professional development, the issue is one of growth along a continuum. This approach offers an inclusive, rather than exclusive, view of teaching adults and children.

Everyone who comes to the field of early childhood education brings some kind of relevant experiences with young children, experiences which form a foundation on which to construct teaching theory and practice. Adults engaged in learning about their profession are usually involved (or should be, as Weikart points out in this volume) with young children in some capacity. All have their own childhoods which provide a beginning point for observing development. In addition, parents have their children's childhoods as an experiential base. People working with children collect new data every day to add to their bank of knowledge.

Teaching is a complex, unpredictable task that requires continual on-the-spot decision making. Decisions are rooted in teachers' theories—and these theories are constructed from experience and practice. After new teachers pass the survival stage, it is shortsighted to train them through a body of social knowledge which, as Piaget has described it (Labinowicz, 1980), is agreed upon by a particular society and taught directly to naive members of that society. Teaching is a more complicated skill than driving, for example, which is largely a combination of physical and social knowledge. Novice drivers practice coordination and memorize rules, and good drivers construct task-related logical knowledge as well. Teaching is never that simple.

Adults as constructivist learners

Competent teachers are autonomous thinkers who must behave like intellectuals. Therefore, constructivist theory offers the best fit to describe the adult learning process, just as it does for young children's learning. The profession is achieving remarkable consensus on the knowledge base of early childhood education, as evidenced in Part II of this book. There is far less agreement on the learning process appropriate to teacher education, although the discussions here bring the field much closer to articulating an understanding.

I have vivid memories of Evangeline Burgess at Pacific Oaks College in the 1950s. She frequently rebelled against the word *training* as it was applied to teacher education. Training, she insisted, is a behaviorist notion in which objectives are set and the beast is shaped through reinforcement.

Education means to draw out, beginning with the learner's own experience, adding new experience, and providing opportunities to reflect and discuss that experience. Evangeline constructed this understanding for herself long before Piaget's ideas caught on.

The words we use don't matter unless we believe them, and many people do keep hoping that teachers can be trained to perform according to expectations. The urge for many teacher educators and staff development specialists is to be efficient fixer-uppers—to tell people what to do, and have them do it. Kamii (1982, 1989) calls this the common-sense view of teaching and learning—and says it's outmoded.

Some who claim to have a more sophisticated view are inclined to teach adults as if they all were at the formal operational level—ready to learn about children simply by listening. This philosophy is contained in the "we have to cover this content" approach. Students and teachers who are facile with abstractions use them to show off, and everyone else in the group waits it out.

A more realistic perspective is to assume that most adults are concrete-operational. Instead of lecturing, adult educators who hold this view work to promote everyone's ability to *tell their stories*. These educators see teaching and learning as storytelling (Jones, 1993) and themselves as facilitators rather than trainers. Facilitation leads to liberation rather than to domestication (Freire, 1970).

A University of Victoria child care training project, designed in collaboration with the Cree and Dene people in northern Saskatchewan balances the introduction of mainstream early childhood education ideas with respect for traditional local child-rearing practices. Margo Greenwood-Church, teaching adults in these communities, found that it didn't work to ask, "What is done in Cree culture?" No one, not even the Elders, would speak for Cree culture as a whole. But they would tell their own stories, for others to learn from if they chose.

Each person's stories are true; they can't be denied. They aren't authority; they're experience. They can be the starting point for reflection and dialogue. Constructivists have pointed out that dialogue among peers is more useful in building understanding than conversation with an authority. Children can genuinely argue with each other, but involvement of an adult "who knows everything" changes the nature of the argument.

Two teacher/writers tell good stories about this process.

- Paley (1986) describes how she learned to stop asking teacher-questions ("Can you guess what I'm thinking?") and, instead, to ask genuine questions and "listen for the answers I could not myself invent."

- Wasserman (1990) describes a sequence she calls play/debrief/replay, in which the teacher's questions are, "What happened?," "What did you notice?" and "What did you think about that?" The data for debriefing come from children's actions with materials and their interactions with peers. The teacher reflects their stories to them and asks for

The urge for many teacher educators and staff development specialists is to be efficient fixer-uppers—to tell people what to do, and have them do it.

more, sometimes adding new, challenging, but still genuine questions to which she does not know the answers.

Growth vs. engineering models

Developmentally appropriate practice in early childhood education is also a good model for effective practice in professional development (Jones, 1986). Adult learners, like children, need to play—to take initiative, make choices among possibilities, act, and interact. Adults also need to go beyond play, to engage in reflection and dialogue about their experiences. Baseline social knowledge (training) may get them started in knowing how to behave, but then adults need continuing opportunities to make intellectual and moral judgments, to observe children's behavior, and to put their experience into words which are taken seriously by other adults—peers and those who lead groups. This process should characterize both college classes and other professional learning experiences. In both settings, *learners should be doing more talking than their instructors do,* and their talk should be based on concrete experience.

This is a growth model, rather than an engineering model (Donmoyer, 1981). It assumes that people are motivated to grow in competence. Some will say that this isn't necessarily true, and it isn't. But if we are working with adult learners, we choose our risks. We can choose to tell people, in detail, what to think and what to do (as most schools do), and risk the possibility that they won't do it if it's not on the test or if no one is watching. Or, we can look for people's points of strength, invite them to describe and explain their work, and gamble on the chance of hooking their interest and getting them to behave like intellectuals in spite of themselves.

It's not possible to take both risks at the same time, but both risks can be sensibly built into early childhood professional development programs. Working in a public/private partnership between Pacific Oaks and the Pasadena Unified School District, I have gotten a clear sense of the balance and useful tension that can be created between fixer-uppers and facilitators (Jones, 1993). Administrators and supervisors are responsible for keeping things fixed up, for using their power to establish a baseline of competence. It's difficult for bosses to facilitate.

But bosses can work cooperatively with people who are free to facilitate—college instructors, consultants, trainers who are outside the program's line of authority—and thus can give priority to nurturing adults as learners. As teachers find their voices and trust themselves to grow, significant changes occur in their behaviors both in and out of classrooms. Facilitators observe and listen, collect and tell stories, and give choices more than they enforce rules. As facilitators, we are modeling appropriate behavior for a teacher's work with children. If, on the other hand, we play expert, we fail to support the disposition toward moral and intellectual autonomy.

Storytelling is a process that helps teachers develop their own voices and gain the skill and confidence in divergent thinking which is necessary to educate children for a changing society. I live in Los Angeles where the

> *Adult learners, like children, need to play—to take initiative, make choices among possibilities, act, and interact. Adults also need to go beyond play, to engage in reflection and dialogue about their experiences.*

1992 riots were one of the countless situations in which people have acted out their anger over injustice. The stories of many diverse people, some of whom have trouble gaining self-respect or hope for the future, are not taken seriously by people in power.

Teachers can't be trained to create riot curriculum; riots aren't in any lesson plan. But in classroom after classroom of California teachers who were engaged in telling their stories, riot curriculum emerged that spring because it was part of those teachers' and children's stories. Sharing stories is an effective way for people—in classrooms and in communities—to learn to solve problems together.

Bibliography

Carter, M., Jones, E., & Lakin, M.B. (1992). *Ideas for staff development*. Pasadena, CA: Pacific Oaks Occasional Papers.

Delpit, L. (1988). The silenced dialogue: Power and pedagogy in educating other people's children. *Harvard Educational Review, 58*(3), 280–298.

Donmoyer, R. (1981). The politics of play. *Journal of Research & Development in Education, 14*(3), 11–18.

Egan, K. (1989). *Teaching as storytelling*. Chicago, IL: University of Chicago Press.

Elbow, P. (1986). *Embracing contraries: Explorations in learning and teaching*. New York: Oxford Press.

Freire, P. (1970). *Pedagogy of the oppressed*. New York: Seabury.

Jones, E. (1986). *Teaching adults: An active-learning approach*. Washington, DC: NAEYC.

Jones, E. (Ed.). (1993). *Growing teachers: Partnerships in staff development*. Washington, DC: NAEYC.

Jones, E., & Reynolds, G. (1992). *The play's the thing: Teachers' roles in children's play*. New York: Teachers College Press.

Kamii, C. (1982). Autonomy as the aim of education: Implications of Piaget's theory. In C. Kamii, *Number in Preschool and Kindergarten* (pp. 73–87). Washington, DC: NAEYC.

Kamii, C. (1989). Leading primary education toward excellence: Beyond worksheets and drill. *Young Children, 40*(6), 3–9.

Paley, V. (1986). On listening to what the children say. *Harvard Educational Review, 56*(2), 122–131.

Wasserman, S. (1990). *Serious players in the primary classroom*. New York: Teachers College Press.

PART IV

Pursuing the Vision of a Professional Development System

Realization of the vision of a coordinated professional development system is drawing closer. Progress—in dismantling some long-standing walls and erecting strong new bridges across the diverse elements of the field—is evident here. When traditional degree and certificate programs are bridged with learning opportunities offered through programs, foundations, community sponsors, and other providers of professional development, the profession will be well on its way toward creation of a sturdy career lattice.

The Center for Career Development in Early Care and Education at Wheelock College, founded by **Gwen Morgan**, concentrates on systematic professional development planning at the state level. The Center's study of the status of training, regulation, and funding in each state is summarized first to provide a comprehensive picture of the myriad of systems and methods that influence early childhood professional development in the United States, and to set the stage for pursuing the vision of a coherent system.

Formulation of state public education policies that promote professional development in the field are critical to a systems approach. **Kenneth E. Nye**, a staff member of the Tennessee State Board of Education, outlines related responsibilities of public policymakers and describes four guidelines that impinge on state policy development in early childhood education.

Many states are currently engaged in planning processes to improve professional development systems. **Andrew J. Stremmel** and **Ann J. Francis**, both from Virginia Polytechnic Institute and State University, outline Virginia's successful process for developing a state plan for professional development, a somewhat unique situation in which the Virginia Affiliate of NAEYC is the lead agency. They describe the information-gathering phase, preliminary recommendations, and most importantly, how other state planning groups can collaborate to develop a comprehensive early childhood professional development system.

Many early childhood educators accumulate a great deal of knowledge about working with young children and their families through on-the-job experience. The values of earning credit for prior learning are presented by **Brenda Fyfe**, director of experiential learning at Webster University. She describes the assessment process and views it as a steppingstone to further professional growth opportunities.

A similar challenge is to achieve reciprocity of credit between two-year and four-year institutions. A brief look at some of the issues discussed at joint sessions of the American Associate Degree Early Childhood Educators (ACCESS) and the National Association of Early Childhood Teacher Educa-

Prospects for unified policy efforts—to strengthen the field's work force and to improve the quality of services—are brighter but must be a major focus of professional development activities.

Early childhood educators who continue to acquire teaching, management, and leadership skills are the most effective change agents for programs and the profession.

tors (NAECTE) during National Institute for Early Childhood Professional Development conferences rounds out the discussion on college credit.

Practical and policy implications of these deliberations conclude this volume, as the focus turns to financing for professional development and compensation of early childhood staff. Professional development and employee compensation are inextricably linked by **Dan Bellm, Terry Gnezda, Marcy Whitebook,** and **Gretchen Stahr Breunig** of the National Center for the Early Childhood Work Force (formerly the Child Care Employee Project). They maintain that prospects for unified policy efforts—to strengthen the field's work force and to improve the quality of services to young children and their families—are brighter but must be a major focus of professional development activities.

Finally, two different approaches to financing are described. The state of Hawaii designed an optimal system for early education and care and then developed strategies to fund this ideal system. This process, described by **Nina Sazer O'Donnell,** consultant to the effort, holds promise for other states. From the ideal we turn to the real, with a description by **Barbara Ferguson Kamara,** head of the D.C. Office of Early Childhood Development, of the financing strategy used in Washington, D.C., which identified and attempted to coordinate all current sources of funding for early childhood professional development.

*   *   *

NAEYC's National Institute for Early Childhood Professional Development prepares leaders to advocate for developmentally appropriate curriculum and assessment, effective teacher preparation across all levels, and the full cost of quality early childhood programs. The Institute works with early childhood professionals at local, state, and national levels to ensure that policy and practices work on behalf of the needs of children and their families. To accomplish this goal, strategic planning and networking—to address early childhood programming and professional development—are crucial. Early childhood educators who continue to acquire teaching, management, and leadership skills are the most effective change agents for programs and the profession.

Future Pursuits: Building Early Care and Education Careers

Gwen Morgan, Sheri L. Azer, Joan B. Costley, Kimberly Elliott, Andrea Genser, Irene F. Goodman, and Bettina McGimsey

The quality of early care and education that children receive depends on the knowledge and skills of the people who care for and teach them—in centers, family child care homes, Head Start programs, and schools. A strong link exists between the quality of care and the specialized training of practitioners. Now more than ever before, the diverse child population in our country needs well-trained practitioners who reflect the cultural, ethnic, and social class heterogeneity of the communities they serve. Moreover, adequate compensation is necessary to attract qualified practitioners to the field and stem the high rate of practitioner turnover, which has a negative effect on the quality of care and education that children receive.

A strong link exists between the quality of care and the specialized training of practitioners.

Making A Career Of It: The State of the States Report on Career Development in Early Care and Education was the most comprehensive national study to collect baseline data, as of 1991, on state policies affecting career development in early care and education. Conducted by The Center for Career Development in Early Care and Education at Wheelock College, the study documented policies that affect the training of practitioners, both those who prepare in advance, before employment, and those who receive specialized training after beginning their work with young children. The study's timing provides baseline data prior to the implementation of the Child Care and Development Block Grant.

Three major policy areas influence practitioner training and career development in the United States:

Regulation. Practitioner qualifications are regulated in the states through two separate processes: licensing and teacher certification. We explored both processes, not to compare them but to form a clear picture of how early childhood practitioners are qualified for their work.

Training opportunities. We surveyed all training options, including both noncredit training—meaning workshops, conferences, and other training that does not carry credit or lead to any type of credential—and credit training, meaning college coursework, certificate or degree programs of credit, or Continuing Education Units that meet national standards.

Financing of training. We studied the use of federal, state, and local public funds for training and private sector funding from foundations and corporations.

To collect information on these policy areas, we gathered data from all states' child care licensing agencies, departments of education, and lead agencies for the Child Care and Development Block Grant, higher education institutions, and key informants. Information was also collected from the District of Columbia and New York City when regulations differed from the states'.

Highlights of major findings

No coordinated system exists across delivery systems to develop well-trained practitioners to work with young children in homes, centers, Head Start programs, and schools.

We found the following:

1. Many early care and education practitioners in America are not required to have any early childhood training to work with young children.

- Early childhood education training prior to employment (known as pre-service training) is not required for child care center teachers in 36 states nor for center directors in 22 states.

- Family child care providers are rarely required to be trained prior to or even after enrolling a small number of children in their homes (see Figure 3).

- Sixteen states have no early childhood teaching certificate or endorsement for public school teachers. In those states a teacher without specific preparation for work with young children is permitted to teach them. Even of the 35 states with early childhood certification, only 21 require experience with children younger than kindergarten age (see Figure 4).

2. Few states set adequate standards for the amount, content, or quality of training.

- Annual ongoing training is the most prevalent form of training required for early childhood practitioners, with the median number being 12 hours per year for caregivers working in centers and 6 hours per year for family and group home child care providers (see Figure 3).

- Fewer than half of the states require specialized training for practitioners to work with infants and toddlers, school-age children, and children with special needs. Administrative training is rarely required for center directors.

3. Licensing and certification place different emphases on experience and training.

- Licensing rules may accept experience in place of academic preparation; teacher certification may accept academic preparation without requiring experience with children younger than age 5.

4. Some states have policies that facilitate career mobility for practitioners.

- Eleven states set qualifications for two levels of roles as center teacher; three states set qualifications for two levels of directors. No state has

Making A Career Of It: The State of the States Report on Career Development in Early Care and Education was a comprehensive national study on state policies affecting career development.

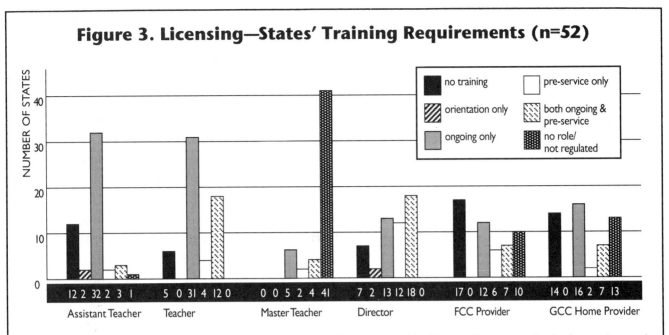

Figure 3. Licensing—States' Training Requirements (n=52)

	Assistant Teacher	Teacher	Master Teacher	Director	FCC Provider	GCC Home Provider
	12 2 32 2 3 1	5 0 31 4 12 0	0 0 5 2 4 41	7 2 13 12 18 0	17 0 12 6 7 10	14 0 16 2 7 13

Legend: no training; pre-service only; orientation only; both ongoing & pre-service; ongoing only; no role/not regulated

Notes: *(1) All data current as of May 1991. (2) Of the three states with Director II, two require both ongoing and preservice training and one requires only ongoing training. (3)* n *includes data on 50 states, Washington, D.C., and New York City.*

Some key report terms

Early care and education—All types of education and care for children from birth through age five and programs for school-age children before and after school and during vacations. We are not suggesting a change in the broadly used definition of birth through age 8 but rather a shift in emphasis for this study.

Practitioners—Individuals currently employed in the field of early care and education.

Training—We use the term *training* generically to cover all specialized preparation for work in early care and education. We believe that all early care and education training should be designed to transform beliefs, perspectives, and behaviors and to contribute to personal growth.

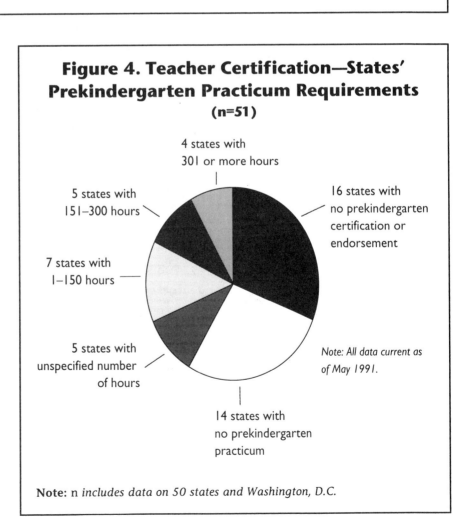

Figure 4. Teacher Certification—States' Prekindergarten Practicum Requirements (n=51)

4 states with 301 or more hours

16 states with no prekindergarten certification or endorsement

5 states with 151–300 hours

7 states with 1–150 hours

5 states with unspecified number of hours

14 states with no prekindergarten practicum

Note: All data current as of May 1991.

Note: n *includes data on 50 states and Washington, D.C.*

Training that develops the full range of essential early care and education knowledge and skills is not consistently available, accessible, or linked coherently.

developed policies to create career mobility for family child care providers.

- Licensing rules favor early access to employment at the expense of pre-service training. Teacher certification favors college degrees at the expense of early accessibility to employment.

5. Child care licensing and teacher certification are separate processes, with no bridges between the two.

- The data showed little joint planning between the two state agencies and few, if any, mechanisms to allow individuals to bridge the two processes.

6. There is a scarcity of training for people working with infants and toddlers or school-age children or for administrators. Equally lacking is training and materials to enable practitioners to work effectively with children and families from diverse ethnic and linguistic groups.

7. Existing college training programs are not always accessible in terms of location, class scheduling, and degree-completion policies to individuals currently employed in early care and education programs.

- Associate degree programs are, in general, significantly more accessible to currently employed practitioners than are bachelor's degree programs, which have traditionally been designed for students preparing for future employment.

- Training is not accessible to early childhood practitioners in rural and remote areas.

8. The various levels of training are not linked.

- Few mechanisms exist to enable practitioners to transform prior non-credit learning experiences and training into credit [e.g., via competency demonstration, mastery credit, or CLEP(Competency Level Evaluation Program)].

- Within higher education, the lack of consistent policies for the transfer and articulation of credits or degrees earned in prior programs or at different institutions presents major barriers to advancement.

9. Public funds to support training are extremely limited, sporadic, and largely uncoordinated.

- Policymakers in few states know the amount that is spent on training in their state.

- Only four of the federal funding sources we identified have funds specifically earmarked for early childhood training: Child Care and Development Block Grant, Child Care Licensing and Improvement Act (not currently funded), Child Development Associate Scholarship, and Head Start. Eleven additional funding sources are applicable on a limited basis for use in training programs for early childhood practitioners.

10. Practitioners and trainers subsidize the true cost of training.

- Many practitioners pay for training out of their limited salaries, and many trainers conduct workshops for little or no pay.

11. Practitioners, administrators, and funders have few incentives to invest in training.

- Low earnings and the perception of the field as a dead-end career make many believe the investment isn't worth it.

*   *   *

In summary, millions of practitioners are not required to have any early childhood training. Training that develops the full range of essential early care and education knowledge and skills is not consistently available, accessible, or linked coherently. Financial support to pursue training is frequently insufficient.

The vision

Our findings gave us a heightened understanding of the complexity of early care and education and the systemic nature of the problems in the field. Regulatory, training delivery, and funding policies are inextricably tied, so altering only one of them will not produce viable, long-term solutions. From our study, we developed and refined a new vision for career development for the field, which consists of five elements:

1. **Systemic planning.** A systems approach involves an understanding of how the parts of the whole—regulation, training delivery, and financing—need to fit together. Many of the problems in early care and education stem from gaps in the system. To improve only one part of the system may create a crisis in another part.

2. **Effective quality controls for the profession.** Qualifications for early childhood roles should reflect the field's knowledge base, ensure skills, be appropriate for specific roles, and be effectively implemented.

3. **Progressive, role-related, appropriate, and articulated training.** Working with young children need not be a dead-end career. A variety of roles exist, but training is essential to help people move into new, increasingly responsible roles. Training should be appropriate to specific roles and child populations and should be offered at different levels of knowledge and skills. Credits from individual courses and certificate and degree programs should count toward, or articulate with, one another. Real access to these opportunities must exist for all people, especially those groups for whom access has been systematically denied, such as low-income individuals and people of color.

4. **Recognition and reward systems.** Increased knowledge and skills in early care and education should be rewarded with increased responsibility, compensation, and status.

5. **Expanded and coordinated financing.** Coordination of funding streams would use limited resources more efficiently. An overall plan for funding of training should place appropriate emphasis on all early care and education practitioners. Funding should be available not only to those pursuing their training prior to employment but also to those who need

Regulatory, training delivery, and funding policies are inextricably tied, so altering only one of them will not produce viable, long-term solutions.

help paying for ongoing career development while employed. Funds should be provided for entry-level training through certificate and degree programs.

Making A Career Of It makes many policy recommendations for planning, regulation, training delivery, and training funding. Among them are the following:

Planning
- *Create a state-level comprehensive planning process* for career development in early care and education.

Regulation
- *Regulate qualifications for a progression of roles* in licensed child care. In centers, include at least two apprentice roles (such as aide and assistant teacher), at least two levels of teachers (teacher and lead or master teacher), and two levels of directors. Set three levels of qualifications for family child care/group child care home providers (such as family child care/group child care home specialist I, II, and III).
- *License individuals* as well as child care facilities.
- *Prohibit experience from being treated as an alternative* to training. Set standards for required experience with an age group: define consistent supervision, qualifications of supervisors, and quality of the program.
- *Define annual ongoing training in both credit and clock hours*, thereby allowing individuals to use this training to meet preservice requirements for more responsible roles.
- *Require substantially more college coursework* for master teachers, directors, and home child care specialist IIIs than for those at the first levels.
- *Require directors* to complete additional coursework in administration.
- *Certify public school prekindergarten teachers* in all states and require a practicum with the age group to which the teacher is assigned.

> *By improving the quality of practitioner preparation, states protect their investment of current dollars and make the most of future investments.*

Training
- *Make training count.* When substantial training of good quality is offered, be sure it carries college credit or can be transformed to college credit that can be applied to certificate or degree programs.
- *Improve access to credit-bearing training* for practitioners who are already employed, particularly people of color and individuals from low-income populations.
- *Articulate programs.* Accept the CDA Credential to count toward an associate degree program; allow the associate degree program to count in full toward a bachelor's degree program.
- *Offer leadership training* assuring greater accessibility for low income populations and people of color.

- *Increase the reimbursement rates in* government subsidy and the expenditure limits in tax credit policies to enable centers and home-based practitioners to charge fees that reflect true costs of quality, improve salaries, and provide incentives for improving quality and staying in the field.
- *Restructure pay schedules* so that income rewards increased training as well as continued work experience. Publish recommended salary scales by role.
- *Allocate 5% of direct service funds to training.* States should total the amount of funds spent on child care and early education from all state and federal sources and allocate 5% of this total for training.

Most of the action to improve the quality of training will have to occur at the state level, with strong federal leadership and support. Policymakers should analyze what changes are needed in their states. Many of these changes will require multiyear efforts. By improving the quality of practitioner preparation, states protect their investment of current dollars and make the most of future investments in early care and education programs for children.

Funding

Morgan, G., Azer, S.L., Costley, J.B., Genser, A., Goodman, I.F., Lombardi, J., & McGimsey, B. (1994). *Making a career of it: The state of the states report on career development in early care and education.* Boston, MA: Center for Career Development in Early Care and Education. (Available from NAEYC. Order #762 [Report]; order #761 [Executive Summary])

Reference

Developing State Early Childhood Education Policies

Kenneth E. Nye

Important to NAEYC's ongoing deliberations on professional development for early childhood educators was the decision in Tennessee to focus the state's teacher credentialing system on results.

Public education policymakers are responsible for setting goals and creating an environment of expectations concerning learning in society. The establishment of state education policy therefore has a great influence on the practical concerns of parents, early childhood educators, and others who support the development of young children and families. For early childhood education, states provide a vision—for new standards of professional excellence and for high-quality programs serving children and families—and opportunities for the vision to emerge.

During the early 1990s, two major policies were adopted in Tennessee that shape the public agenda for early childhood programs in the state and provide a framework within which state agencies, community organizations, early childhood educators, and parents can develop comprehensive, quality programs and related activities for young children and their families. Four aspects of policy development were key to the formulation of these policies and are relevant for consideration by other states engaged in the same processes.

Policies that shape the agenda

Staff qualifications, as regulated by teacher licensure standards, and the requirements for programs set by child care program licensing regulations serving young children are the two primary state policies that shape early childhood programs and professional preparation for individuals working in the field.

Teacher licensure standards. New state standards for licensing teachers evolved as part of Tennessee's 1984 education reforms. The State Board of Education, along with the Tennessee Higher Education Commission and State Certification Commission, were directed to review the status of teacher education programs in the state and to establish new policies and priorities for teacher preparation programs. The review resulted in a comprehensive teacher education policy adopted by the State Board of Education in January 1988.

This new policy required the development of a number of specific implementation activities. Among these are new teacher licensure standards for the various teaching endorsement areas issued by the state on a license to teach. Important to NAEYC's ongoing deliberations on professional development for early childhood educators was the decision in Tennessee to focus the state's teacher credentialing system on results. Licensure standards were expressed in terms of what teachers need to know and be able to do. Approval of teacher preparation programs at higher education institutions in the state is shifted to a thorough review of each program's capabilities to prepare teachers and a focus on the performance of program graduates.

In Tennessee, a State Advisory Council on Teacher Education and Certification developed standards and guidelines for teacher education programs and teacher licensure. Early in its deliberations, the Advisory Council recognized the need to address the area of teacher licensure for early childhood education because schools and community agencies continued to expand the number of programs for young children. The new standards which were recommended by the Advisory Council and adopted by the State Board of Education provided an early childhood education teaching endorsement (pre-kindergarten through third grade) and a special education pre-school or early childhood teaching endorsement (pre-kindergarten through first grade). The state did not previously license teachers in either of these teaching areas.

Program requirements. The second Tennessee policy that shaped program decisions for young children was a comprehensive statement on the development and implementation of early childhood education and parent involvement programs. This policy was developed to support the Master Plan for Tennessee Schools adopted by the State Board of Education and Governor Ned McWherter's education goals for the 21st century. Both documents focused on ensuring that all low-income children would have the opportunity to participate in early childhood education programs. The early childhood education and parent involvement policy went further by describing the requirements for all public school programs serving young children and families regardless of economic status or the source of program funding.

The following four aspects were important to the early childhood education policy development approach in Tennessee:
- Articulation of the early childhood education program principles to be reinforced and enacted in state policy.
- Understanding the shift of support structures for children and families that early childhood education policy must address.
- Changing the perspective of policymakers on how public services should be structured and delivered—from bureaucratic to responsive systems.
- Recognizing the education policy instruments at a state level that can be used to create change and improvement in early childhood education programs.

Articulate ECE principles. The first guideline for policy development was articulation of the early childhood education program principles to be reinforced and enacted in policy. Providing clarification and focus on key ideas was important not only for shaping the final policy, but for guiding the specific program development that would follow. These nine program principles were identified, and then reinforced and enacted, in Tennessee's early childhood education policy.
- Early childhood education programs that are quality, comprehensive,

Providing clarification and focus on key ideas was important not only for shaping the final policy, but for guiding the specific program development that would follow.

Guidelines for policy development

and community-based must be supported and recognized by public schools because of the immediate benefit for schools as well as families.

- Early childhood education professional preparation and program services must address the developmental age span from birth through 8 years of age.

- Early childhood education programs must be developmentally appropriate in their design and implementation.

- Early childhood education program services must be comprehensive and address all aspects of a child's development.

- Early childhood education programs must be family focused and include the total family unit in designing and implementing program support services and activities.

- Training standards for early childhood education program staff should be based upon the recognized knowledge and skills required to work with young children and their families, and the standards should reinforce and emphasize quality, comprehensive service delivery.

- Early childhood education programs should be locally formulated and community based in the delivery of services.

- Early childhood education programs must seek out interagency collaboration in the design and delivery of the program.

- Early childhood education programs must promote a partnership between parents, schools, and communities that doesn't stop at the schoolhouse door. In essence, as the National Association of State Boards of Education recommended, the creation of an early childhood unit is required.

Family support structures. Social indicators clearly point to a shift in the traditional support structure for children and families. The triad of extended family, neighborhood, and church has evolved toward a support structure of nuclear family, schools, and community, although this shift can not be easily characterized for all communities, and it is not uniform for all children and families. Easily interpreted descriptions of the dynamics of this shift are needed by state policymakers to use in policy decisions affecting children and families (Figure 5).

Restructured public services. Perspectives on how public services should be structured and delivered by government are changing (Carr & Littman, 1990; Osborne & Gaebler, 1992). State and local government units are moving toward a more responsive system, and away from the bureaucratic top-down approach. Managing quality in an environment of international competition for resources is part of that perspective. It is important for early childhood educators and those who shape policy in this area to recognize these changes. *Reinventing Government* (Osborne & Gaebler, 1992) describes these changes:

> Today's environment demands institutions that are extremely flexible and adaptable. It demands institutions that deliver high-quality goods and services, squeezing ever more bang out of every buck. It demands institu-

Easily interpreted descriptions are needed by state policymakers to use in policy decisions affecting children and families.

Figure 5. Changing Support Structures for Children and Families

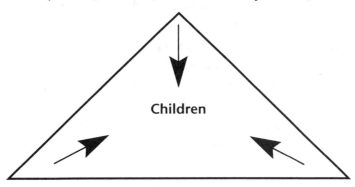

Extended Family
(Parents, relatives, and close family friends)

Children

Neighborhood
(School, friends, and neighbors)

Church
(Social services, youth organizations,
social and spiritual nurturance)

TRADITIONAL SUPPORT STRUCTURE

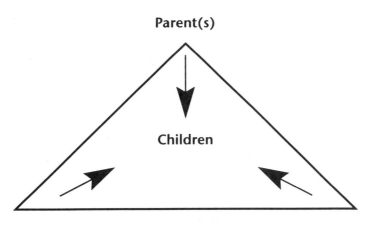

Parent(s)

Children

Community
(Church, community youth organizations,
social service organizations, and
neighborhood, and family acquaintances)

School
(Extended family functions)

EVOLVING SUPPORT STRUCTURE

State and local government units are moving toward a more responsive system, and away from the bureaucratic top-down approach.

tions that are responsive to their customers, offering choices of nonstandardized services; that lead by persuasion and incentives rather than commands; that give their employees a sense of meaning and control, even ownership. It demands institutions that empower citizens rather than simply serving them. (Osborne & Gaebler, 1992)

Instruments of change. The fourth step important to state policy development is to recognize the policy instruments that can create improvement and change in programs for young children. Early childhood education programs are primarily concerned with supporting typical development of children and families, so the field over time has become more closely aligned with education and social welfare policy. However, the medical profession provides one model of multi-level staffing, training, and service delivery.

In public education and social welfare, there are four primary policy instruments available at the state level that provide an opportunity to promote and support professional development and improved program quality in early childhood education.

- **Licensing or certifying education personnel**
    Teaching endorsement areas
    Knowledge and skills required for licensing/certification
- **Approving formal preparation programs leading to licensure or certification of education personnel**
    Program approval standards
    Procedures and processes for approval of programs
- **Approving or licensing early childhood education programs** (i.e., schools, preschools, and child care programs)
    Employment standards
    Professional development programs and processes
    Program licensing or approval standards
- **Establishing state funding levels for programs and the funding processes**
    Supporting diversification of programs
    Promoting the continuing growth and development of programs
    Supporting professional development mechanisms

Working together, policymakers and early childhood educators can establish a framework that supports the goals of professional development and addresses the needs of young children and their families for quality program services.

Carr, D., & Littman, I. (1990). *Excellence in government.* Arlington, VA: Coopers & Lybrand.

National Association of State Boards of Education. (1988). *Right from the start: The report of the NASBE Task Force on Early Childhood Education.* Alexandria, VA: Author.

Osborne, D., & Gaebler, T. (1992). *Reinventing government.* Reading, MA: Addison-Wesley.

Tennessee State Board of Education. (1989). *Special education: Preschool/ early childhood teacher licensure standards (PreK–1).* Nashville, TN: Author.

Tennessee State Board of Education. (1990). *Early childhood education teacher licensure standards (Pre-K–3).* Nashville, TN: Author.

Tennessee State Board of Education. (1991a). *Master plan for Tennessee schools.* Nashville, TN: Author.

Tennessee State Board of Education. (1991b). *Policy for early childhood education and parent involvement in Tennessee.* Nashville, TN: Author.

Bibliography

Collaborating on a State Plan for Professional Development

Andrew J. Stremmel and Ann J. Francis

Research has established a strong relationship between formal education in child development/early childhood education and effective performance with young children (Arnett, 1989; Howes, 1983; Howes, Whitebook, & Phillips, 1983; Ruopp, Travers, Glantz, & Coelen, 1979). Yet, as discussion in this volume documents, the early childhood profession lacks a collective mechanism to upgrade the knowledge and skills of staff, and most states require only minimal preparation for center- and home-based caregivers (Morgan et al., 1994; Phillips, Lande, & Goldberg, 1990).

The lack of a coherent and systematic plan for initial and continuous professional development of early childhood personnel led to a number of national and state initiatives, including NAEYC's National Institute for Early Childhood Professional Development (Dorsey, 1993). The major assumption underlying these efforts is that increased levels of knowledge will lead to improved service quality and enhanced status and salaries of early childhood personnel.

Recognizing the need for a more effective and coordinated system of training in the state of Virginia, a number of organizations joined forces to develop a comprehensive plan.

Recognizing the need for a more effective and coordinated system of training in the state of Virginia, a number of organizations joined forces in January 1992 to begin the process of developing a comprehensive plan for professional early childhood teacher preparation and development. The Virginia Plan is unique in that, even though funding for the project came from Child Care and Development Block Grant funds, the lead organization in developing the plan was the Virginia Association for Early Childhood Education (VAECE), an NAEYC Affiliate Group. The process—long-term, continuous, collaborative, and inclusive of all stakeholders in the early childhood community—is described here.

The process

In 1990 the Virginia Department of Social Services and the Virginia Council on Child Day Care and Early Childhood Programs issued a request for proposals to develop a comprehensive state professional development plan. Excitement and curiosity about the project was widespread and a number of organizations considered competing for the grant. A small group of individuals who were affiliated with these organizations recognized the need for collaboration and decided to seek approval from their groups to submit a proposal as a coalition. The steering committee included VAECE, the Virginia Child Care Resource and Referral Network (VACCRRN), the Early Childhood Development Coalition (ECDC) of the Virginia Community College system, and the Child Development faculty at Virginia Polytechnic Institute and State University. A grant of $20,000 was awarded to the team, with VAECE serving as the lead agency.

Collaboration was achieved on many levels. In addition to cooperation between two state agencies and the initial coalition, the need for broader representation was recognized. An advisory committee, designed to reflect the diverse elements of the field, was formed by the funding agencies to oversee the project. In January 1992, with the first meeting of the advisory committee, the project officially began.

Information gathering. Data gathering about early childhood professional development was the first major task toward developing a comprehensive plan. The steering committee contracted with the Center for Career Development in Early Care and Education at Wheelock College to provide an overview of national trends and progress in other states. Steering committee members collected information about the history and status of early childhood professional development in Virginia. Individuals and local organizations that provide professional development opportunities for practitioners were surveyed. Parents who used resource and referral (R & R) services were interviewed to obtain information about their priorities for professional preparation of early childhood educators working with their children.

Representation and cooperation from all segments of the early childhood community are necessary to overcome obstacles to an articulated professional development system (Bredekamp, 1992; Costley, 1991). Therefore, focus groups and strategic planning sessions were held to obtain information from a diverse group of child care providers and statewide organizations that provide early childhood professional development. These sessions were considered essential to the process of developing a truly inclusive, coordinated system. Focus groups, in particular, made it possible to include a large number of unlicensed family child care providers and religiously-exempt center caregivers in the process. The most valuable information was obtained from these meetings, and is highlighted here because it formed the basis for many of the final recommendations.

The Virginia Plan is unique in that the lead organization in developing the plan was the Virginia Association for Early Childhood Education (VAECE), an NAEYC Affiliate.

Focus groups and strategic planning. Focus group meetings involved anyone who wished to participate, and included staff and directors from child care, nursery school, school-age, and recreation programs, as well as family child care providers. They were held in four areas of the state, with separate sessions for family child care providers, program administrators, and program staff. Issues and concerns were discussed related to training availability, affordability, coordination, incentives, suitability, and qualifications of trainers.

Practitioners had very different needs, depending on whether they were from rural or urban areas. Most felt that a combination of training and experience in the classroom should be considered when being evaluated for salary increases. The best staff development leaders were seen as people who had not only expertise, but classroom experience. One family child care provider told us that she and her colleagues did not want "briefcase people," people who come in with a briefcase full of research but no practical knowledge of how the information applies to young children.

After completion of the focus groups, three strategic planning sessions

One family child care provider told us that she and her colleagues did not want "briefcase people" who come in with a briefcase full of research but no practical knowledge.

were held at central locations to build strong alliances and promote coordination among institutions of higher education and other training providers. Each meeting lasted two days, with meals and lodging expenses covered for all participants. Invitations were sent through the office of the Secretary of Health and Human Services to individuals in two- and four-year-college early childhood programs, U.S.D.A. Food Program sponsor agencies, R & R agencies, the Virginia Cooperative Extension System, and professional organizations.

Approximately 60 individuals took part in sessions facilitated by Joan Costley from the Center for Career Development at Wheelock, and Joan Lombardi, an early childhood specialist. These individuals were chosen because they were recognized experts with no political stake in the outcome of the project. Discussion centered on what a system of professional development in Virginia would look like, and how the goals set for this system might be achieved. Questions such as credentialing of practitioners and trainers, coordination of professional development programs in the community, the relationship between early childhood and public schools, and problems with transfer of credits between institutions were discussed. Many more questions were created from these discussions, and participants expressed interest in continuing the planning process beyond the first year. They recognized that the issues were too complex to solve in six days of meetings.

Major findings

Four recurring themes emerged in the review of Virginia's professional development resources, delivery mechanisms, and funding streams:

- Lack of funding for professional development.
- Lack of a reliable statewide data base, due to the absence of a stable, universal system for collecting and defining data.
- Lack of coordination among agencies and institutions that provide professional development opportunities.
- Inconsistency of availability, accessibility, affordability, and quality of professional development opportunities for providers.

Based on these findings, and in response to concerns and ideas generated by the focus groups, strategic planning sessions, and feedback from the advisory committee, interim and long-range recommendations were developed.

Summary of recommendations

Short-term recommendations addressed the areas of coordination and availability of professional development opportunities. These included initiatives such as development of a statewide event calendar and coordination of efforts conducted by the Division of Licensing Programs, Head Start, and others that receive public funding. Other recommendations included formation of a statewide data base to receive input from R & R agencies about opportunities and demand, staff development on specific topic areas, and funding in various localities.

Both the steering and advisory committees strongly recommended that the planning process be continued, with a state-level representative advisory committee overseeing the process. Task forces were requested to study credentialing of practitioners and trainers, higher education, coordination of delivery systems, and public funding for professional development.

Long-term recommendations called for an overall system driven by the field, with the formation of a statewide institute for professional development. Members of the institute would be appointed by organizations representing practitioners, higher education, and individuals and groups providing specialized and continuous training. The model is based on the assumption that standards for professional development should be set by those who are in the field, and that certification or accreditation programs should be likewise governed by the profession. This private, nonprofit institute would cooperate with state government to coordinate the training system, and would contract with state government to fund the system, but might also seek other funding. It would also set policy for the system. Regional coalitions would be the local arms of the system, with localities determining their own professional development needs and priorities.

The model is based on the assumption that standards for professional development should be set by those who are in the field, and that certification or accreditation programs should be likewise governed by the profession.

Lessons learned from the process

Documentation is difficult. Although a large amount of information has been generated by numerous studies on early childhood education in Virginia, few of the recommendations have been implemented. One reason became painfully evident during the data collection process. There is no easy and reliable way to obtain information on who is conducting professional development activities, who is receiving them, and where they are being conducted. Consequently, collecting reliable and convincing evidence that can inform the policy decisions required to implement a comprehensive model is a very difficult task.

Decisions are influenced by many factors. Another reason that previous recommendations failed to impact major program initiatives is that research findings ignore the political, social, and economic forces that influence policy decisions (Haskins & Adams, 1983). As the professional development of early childhood educators becomes a more urgent and understood need within the field and by the public, and as early childhood researchers and advocates develop a clearer sense of direction, policies that facilitate the process of professionalization are more likely to be formulated.

Visions change. Perhaps the most sobering realization gained from the process is that the vision the project's leaders had at the beginning was destined to change significantly over the course of its implementation. Some of the project's expectations were unrealistic. Initial goals were scaled back, and the group accepted a multi-year project. A multi-phased approach, with a longer and more realistic timeline, was adopted. Phase one of the process is described here.

In phase two, some interim recommendations are being implemented,

A family child care provider, drove two hours through snow to a focus group meeting. She was determined to let her voice be heard.

such as the formation and meeting of task forces and the advisory committee, investigation of funding, and development of a statewide training calendar. Phase three, expected to be complete by the year 2000, is full implementation of the professional development system throughout the state.

Early childhood professional development is different. Throughout the process of developing this plan, it was necessary to keep in mind that early childhood is conceptually different in focus than traditional (i.e., medical) models of professional development (Bredekamp & Willer, 1993). The early childhood model must be as responsive and dynamic as the field for which it is intended, and it must be based on the assumption that standards for professional development should be set by people in the field. Input from practitioners is essential. One woman, a family child care provider, drove two hours through snow to a focus group meeting. She was determined to let her voice be heard.

Collaboration brings new perspectives. Having the right people at the table is crucial. Those who represent organizations must be invested in the collaborative process, must be knowledgeable about the issues, and must have education and experience in the field. Additionally, they must be willing to share the work and the credit, and they must believe that they have a stake in the process.

Including all stakeholders may be threatening, but is rewarding in the long run because those who participate are more likely to buy into the plan. For example, one participant in the strategic planning process stated that her organization did not believe that its views would be considered or valued, but she was convinced otherwise in the course of the planning process.

Because the collaborative process enabled everyone's voices to be heard, it was possible to consider a variety of perspectives. Continuous evaluation, expansion, and reevaluation of proposals and ideas for components of the plan occurred as a result. This system of checks and balances is important. For example, the steering committee was focusing more on long-range recommendations for a system. The advisory committee helped steering committee members realize that interim recommendations that could be readily implemented were also needed, so that coordination of current funds and programs could begin. Participation of individuals in public and private sectors, within and outside state government, helps retain the focus on long-term goals.

Obtain outside, objective assistance. Having facilitators with no political stake in the outcome, but who are accepted as credible leaders by all parties, takes much of the threat and suspicion out of the process.

Starting the process

Individuals in the early childhood community who want to become involved in planning for professional development in their states are offered these suggestions to get started:

1. **Find out who the players are.** Contact agencies such as the state child care licensing office or department of education to find out if planning efforts are underway. If so, get on the mailing list, attend focus group meetings, express interest in becoming involved. If not, try to find out who provides most of the training for child care providers and who might have an interest in beginning the planning process. Contact professional organizations and associations to see who is interested in professional development. Contact institutions of higher education, including community colleges and four-year colleges and universities that have early childhood departments or prepare early childhood practitioners.

2. **Find out where the money is.** Find out who the Child Care and Development Block Grant (CCDBG) lead agency is. Ask who is paying for training in the state and where they receive their funding. Ask colleges whether there are funds to help students who take early childhood classes or continuing education workshops.

3. **Encourage collaboration.** Be willing to share credit and assist in developing a planning project. Offer skills and resources and ask others what they can bring to the project. Work with leaders and decision makers of various organizations and agencies.

Including all stakeholders may be threatening, but is rewarding in the long run because those who participate are more likely to buy into the plan.

4. **Investigate what other states are doing.** Attend NAEYC's National Institute for Early Childhood Professional Development conferences and contact The Center for Career Development in Early Care and Education at Wheelock College in Boston for the most current information about national trends in planning for professional development systems.

5. **Be persistent, patient, and prudent.** Work collaboratively with others to develop a proposal to present to agencies that have funding and are most interested in training. Suggest cooperation and coordination across agencies. Be sure to carefully research who the right players are and invite their participation. Expect the project to take time. Do not try to produce a quick report without thinking of the long-term implications.

The process of a statewide collaborative effort to develop a comprehensive early childhood professional development system certainly has its challenges. The Virginia plan will continue to change and grow with the profession and the children for whom this work is aimed.

References

Arnett, J. (1989). Caregivers in day care centers: Does training matter? *Journal of Applied Developmental Psychology, 19*, 541–552.

Bredekamp, S. (1992). The early childhood profession coming together. *Young Children, 47*(6), 36–39.

Bredekamp, S., & Willer, B. (1993). Professionalizing the field of early childhood education: Pros and cons. *Young Children, 48*(3), 82–84.

Costley, J. (1991). *Career development systems in early child care and educa-*

tion: A planning approach. Center for Career Development in Early Care and Education, Boston, MA.

Dorsey, A.G. (1993). Preparation of staff for early childhood settings. *Child & Youth Care Forum, 21*(6), 415–425.

Haskins, R., & Adams, D. (1983). *Parent education and public policy.* New Jersey: Ablex.

Howes, C. (1983). Caregiver behavior in center and family day care. *Journal of Applied Developmental Psychology, 4,* 99–107.

Howes, C., Whitebook, M., & Phillips, D. (1993) Teacher characteristics and effective teaching in child care: Findings from the National Child Care Staffing Study. *Child & Youth Care Forum, 21*(6), 399–414.

Morgan, G., Azer, S.L., Costley, J.B., Elliott, K., Genser, A., Goodman, I.F., & McGimsey, B. (1994). Future pursuits: Building early care and education careers. *Young Children, 49*(3), 80–83.

Phillips, D., Lande, J., & Goldberg, M. (1990). The state of child care regulation: A comparative analysis. *Early Childhood Research Quarterly, 5,* 151–179.

Ruopp, R., Travers, J., Glantz, R., & Coelen, C. (1979). *Children at the center: Final results of the National Day Care Study.* Cambridge, MA: ABT Associates.

Coordination of this project was a joint effort of many individuals, including Marsha G. Protinsky and Ellen A Tuyahov, who served as members of the Steering Committee, Peggy O. Harrelson and Catherine A. Loveland, Project Managers, and members of the Training Plan Advisory Committee.

Assessing Experiential Learning for College Credit

Brenda Fyfe

Higher education is responding to the influx of adult learners seeking degrees by extending hours and developing new services to accommodate nontraditional learners. One of these new services is assessment of prior learning. This process recognizes that most people engage in informal learning throughout their lives and that such learning, through fair and reliable evaluation procedures, may be of sufficient depth to result in the award of college credit (Lamdin, 1992).

According to a Council for Adult and Experiential Learning (CAEL) survey, more than 1,400 U.S. colleges and universities offer some form of assessment of prior learning for college credit (Fugate & Chapman, 1992). This opportunity may enable many non-degreed early childhood educators to move along the field's career lattice more quickly. The process enables individuals to gain recognition for what they already know, and can open the door to college study at a more appropriate level of competence. The reflection required for assessment is in itself a growth-promoting experience.

Prior learning assessment is the process by which experiential learning is identified, evaluated, and equated with an amount of college credit (Knapp & Jacobs, 1981). It is not credit for years of experience or positions held or workshops attended. Prior learning assessment focuses on college-level learning outcomes because "when credit is granted for input rather than outcomes, the assessment process is short-circuited and credit is given for experience rather than for learning" (Whitaker, 1989, p. 6).

Experience and learning are not equivalent (Dewey, 1938). Most experience results in some kind of learning, but it may not be college-level learning or meet professional standards. The emphasis in higher education is on understanding the meaning and knowledge a student has constructed from experience. An early childhood educator can work in the field for a long time, attend a variety of workshops, and follow program policies, but still not necessarily understand the principles of developmentally appropriate practice. Conversely, a teacher in a program that encourages staff to discuss, share, examine, and question information obtained through training or in working with children and families, may gain a great deal of understanding about principles of early childhood education.

Standards for assessment. The prior learning assessment process identifies areas in which individuals have constructed college-level knowledge, gaps in that knowledge, and college course work that best meets the needs of the student. Standards for assessing learning are defined by Whitaker (1989):

Experience and learning are not equivalent. Most experience results in some kind of learning, but it may not be college-level learning or meet professional standards.

Prior learning assessment

- Credit for experience should be awarded only for learning, and not for experience.
- Credit should be awarded only for college-level learning.
- Credit should be awarded only for learning that has a balance between theory and practical application.
- The determination of competence levels and of credit awards must be made by appropriate subject matter and academic experts.
- Credit should be appropriate to meet the academic context in which it is accepted. (p.xvii)

*Early childhood educators are more likely to obtain credit through **individualized assessment** by performance-based or written challenge exams, or portfolio review.*

Whitaker's book also establishes the general principles of good practice that enhance the likelihood of meeting the standards.

Assessment methods. Credit for prior learning can be earned in a variety of ways, and colleges and universities differ with regard to the options they accept. The most common form of assessment is **standardized testing** such as that offered by the College Level Examination Program (CLEP) and the American College Testing Proficiency Examination Program (ACT PEP). These tests address liberal arts, business management, and nursing. Early childhood staff with knowledge in these areas may choose to take exams for the purpose of accumulating elective or general studies credit if the credits fit into the student's degree plan. ACT PEP offers four exams in education (one in educational psychology and three in reading instruction). The only CLEP exam that relates to the early childhood education knowledge base is on human growth and development.

Many adults are educated through courses sponsored by the military, corporations, unions, and government agencies. The American Council on Education (ACE) evaluates many of these courses through its **Program on Non-Collegiate Sponsored Instruction** (PONSI). Few if any of the assessed

Assessment of prior learning for college credit may enable many non-degreed early childhood educators to move along the field's career lattice more quickly.

programs relate to early childhood education, although credit may apply toward electives or general studies. Students attending colleges that accept ACE-evaluated courses need only document completion of the course(s) in order to receive credit.

Some colleges and universities have **articulation agreements** with proprietary schools or local corporations that offer training. Students who have completed such programs may be able to receive transfer credit upon submission of appropriate documentation.

Early childhood educators are more likely to obtain credit through **individualized assessment** by performance-based or written challenge exams, or portfolio review. Results of the CAEL survey indicated that many institutions understand the appropriateness of these options (Fugate & Chapman, 1992). Challenge exams are available at some colleges for specific courses. A performance-based examination and/or oral interview may be conducted as well.

Portfolio assessment usually allows for the broadest array of content areas to be assessed. It requires a great deal of reflection and self-assessment. These two excerpts from student handbooks capture the essence and value of this process:

- "A portfolio represents you and your college-level learning. It serves as a medium of communicating between you and the faculty experts who will be interviewing you and making decisions about credit awards." (Webster University)

- "Regardless of the number of credits actually awarded, the process can be beneficial in helping you to assess your educational level and to integrate past learning with present college study. Also, by systematically identifying, evaluating, and communicating your prior learning experiences, you are better prepared to provide valid information to others in proving what you know and can do." (Johnson County [Missouri] Community College)

Mandell and Michelson (1990) point out the value-added nature of portfolio preparation and assessment:

> The reflective dimension is valuable even in cases in which student's prior knowledge is not creditable as college-level learning. In cases of paraprofessional work, for example, the nature and structure of a student's knowledge may lack the systematic theoretical framework required of academic learning. Yet the student's workplace history may still have fostered important analytical and decision-making skills. The opportunity to reflect on and articulate the successful acquisition of skills in the past can build confidence and pride even when it does not lead to a credit award. (p. 3)

The formatting of portfolios differs from one institution to another, but written materials usually include articulation of learning outcomes, reflections on related experience, and documentation for each area of learning to be assessed. A credit or noncredit course may be provided to teach students how to prepare the portfolio.

Early childhood educators who aspire to complete a college degree may find that assessment of prior learning is an enabling process.

College faculty members with appropriate subject matter and academic expertise assess the portfolio to determine competence levels and credit awards. Transcripts indicating credit for prior learning assessment communicate particular skill or knowledge competence, rather than a block of credit for experiential learning (Whitaker, 1989). Credit awards may not duplicate any other college credit on the student's transcript.

Restrictions. Most colleges establish policies with regard to limits on the amount of assessed credit that may be applied toward the degree or major, treatment of the credit as transfer or residency credit, and prerequisites (e.g., the student must be seeking a degree, or a minimum number of credit hours must be earned at the institution before eligibility for the assessment process). Assessment charges vary, but usually are much less expensive than tuition for equivalent college courses.

Conclusions

Early childhood educators who aspire to complete a college degree may find that assessment of prior learning is an enabling process. Students can move more quickly toward their goals, gain official recognition for experiential learning, and enroll in course work that fits with their knowledge levels. When an assessment program follows principles of good practice (Whitaker, 1989), students and faculty can be assured that assessed credit is a legitimate part of a college education.

References

Dewey, J. (1938). *Experience and education.* New York: Macmillan.

Fugate, M., & Chapman, R. (1992). *Prior learning assessment: Results of a nationwide institutional survey.* Chicago: Council for Adult and Experiential Learning.

Knapp, J., & Jacobs, P. (1981). *Setting standards for assessing experiential learning.* Englewood Cliffs, NJ: Prentice-Hall.

Lamdin, L. (1992). *Earn college credit for what you know* (2nd ed.). Chicago: Council for Adult and Experiential Learning.

Mandell, A., & Michelson, E. (1990). *Portfolio development and adult learning: Purposes and strategies.* Chicago: Council for Adult and Experiential Learning.

Whitaker, U. (1989). *Assessing learning: Standards, principles, and procedures.* Chicago: Council for Adult and Experiential Learning.

Articulation Issues Facing Two-Year and Four-Year Programs

American Associate Degree Early Childhood Educators (ACCESS) and National Association of Early Childhood Teacher Educators (NAECTE)

The lack of articulation among programs at different levels is a significant barrier to upward professional development. Articulation is partly a territorial and partly an economic issue in which senior institutions refuse to accept professional preparation obtained at another institution. However, the "different" levels of credit are an additional problem. It is impossible for an associate-degree program to offer coursework at the junior or senior level, and the trend is toward fifth year-programs of study. (Bredekamp, 1991, p. 37)

In a historic first meeting, the National Association of Early Childhood Teacher Educators (NAECTE) and the American Associate Degree Early Childhood Educators (ACCESS) came together at the Institute's 1992 conference (and again in 1993) to discuss issues regarding articulation between teacher preparation programs at the associate and baccalaureate degree levels.

These discussion questions were used to help participants focus on the issues, seek alternative ways to work together, appreciate the roles that both institutions can play, and improve communication throughout higher education. The questions can be used to begin similar dialogues between institutions at the state level.

These questions focus on the issues, seek alternative ways to work together, appreciate the roles that both institutions can play, and improve communication throughout higher education.

1. What has the state done about articulation issues? What worked? What didn't?

2. How can the field grapple with different career goals among prospective early childhood practitioners? What about changing career goals and route changes?

3. How can four-year programs respond to sandwiching (pressure to devote the initial four years to liberal arts with a fifth year for professional studies) and pressure for articulation with two-year programs? How do two-year and four-year institutions respond to the greater emphasis in higher education on the liberal arts?

4. What do faculty at four-year institutions need to understand about the academic, social, and cultural environment from which transfer students emerge?

5. What academic skills developed in two-year programs seem to be essential to successful transfer?

6. What forms of support in two-year and four-year colleges are needed for students who are encouraged to raise their aspirations and continue their education?

7. How can faculty best assist transfer students as they face adjustment

challenges? What are the adjustment challenges they typically face? What expectations need to be clarified?

8. How can educators more fully inform students about transfer goals, policies, and procedures?

9. Can computerized transfer guides be developed to aid evaluation of transfer credits?

10. Minority students make up 30% of community college enrollment but are least likely to continue their education at four-year institutions. How might the transfer process be improved for minority students? What extra help might they need to negotiate the transfer process?

11. Originally, the primary mission of two-year colleges was to offer students the first two years of a liberal arts education. Does the occupational orientation stressed by community colleges in the past 15 years limit possibilities for transfer of courses in academic areas? Should occupational programs be re-oriented so that more courses count as liberal arts courses? Are there better ways to coordinate liberal arts requirements?

12. If no more than 25% of community college students transfer to four-year institutions, could a stronger focus on the transfer function jeopardize the diverse ends serviced by a more comprehensive community college philosophy?

13. How can two-year and four-year college faculty work together to better articulate their programs with respect to state and national standards for early childhood professional development?

Barriers and solutions to articulation fell into three categories: structural, fiscal, and communication.

Building bridges for articulation

Barriers and solutions identified by the group fell into three categories: structural, fiscal, and communication. Some of their perspectives are included here.

Barriers to articulation

Structural

- Equivalency problems in the transfer of liberal education requirements and professional education requirements.
- "Sandwiching" of four-year programs by demands from two-year programs and demands of teacher education reform for liberal arts and fifth-year programs.
- Restraints imposed by state certification standards or the National Council for the Accreditation of Teacher Education (NCATE).

Fiscal

- Lack of funds and/or time to evaluate programs or coursework.
- Competition for field placements.
- Perceived loss of credits at four-year institutions if all two-year credits are accepted.

Communication

- Turf issues regarding what courses and which students belong to each institution.
- Lack of knowledge about what each institution is really teaching.

- Perceptions about how much of the knowledge base is offered at either institution.

Structural

- Use NCATE requirements and NAEYC's guidelines for teacher preparation at the baccalaureate and advanced levels in the design of programs at the associate degree level.
- Develop reciprocity or full articulation agreements, that is, the acceptance of an identified set of courses.
- Establish compatible entrance requirements.
- Provide remediation to increase the prospects for student success at both institutions.
- Focus on the transition of students, including those from a variety of cultural, ethnic, or socioeconomic backgrounds.
- Monitor program and course quality to ensure that credits are of equal value.

Fiscal

- Publish models of articulation that work.
- Use common field sites and observe students from each preparation program.
- Conduct mutual advising for students who will transfer.

Communication

- Include faculty from both groups in consortium arrangements.
- Arrange for visiting faculty at each institution or faculty teams from both institutions.
- Develop communication networks.
- Adopt a "student service" attitude.

Alaska, Connecticut, Hawaii, Illinois, Maryland, New Mexico, Pennsylvania, and West Virginia are among the states that have begun to identify and address the challenges and possible solutions to articulation at one or more levels. Strategies include the development of higher education consortia, legislation, and policy that supports articulation agreements.

Possible solutions to articulation

Bibliography

Bredekamp, S. (1991). A vision for early childhood professional development. *Young Children, 47*(1), 35–37.

California State Postsecondary Education Commission. (1990). *Transfer and articulation in the 1990s: California in the larger picture.* Sacramento, CA: Author. (ERIC Document Reproduction Service No. ED 338 200)

Cross, K.P. (1990). *Transfer: Major mission of community colleges?* Paper presented at the Annual International Conference on Leadership Development of the League for Innovation in Community Colleges, San Francisco.

Hatfield, S., & Stewart, D. (1988). Stamping out the transfer run-around. *Educational Record, 69,* 50–53.

National Center for Academic Achievement and Transfer. (1991). *Setting* the national agenda: Academic achievement and transfer education. *Washington, DC: American Council on Education. (ERIC Document Reproduction Service No. ED 336 138)

Watkins, B.T. (1989). Community colleges urged to bolster liberal arts to help students transfer. *Chronicle of Higher Education, 36*(9), A35, A38.

Watkins, B.T. (1990). Two-year institutions under pressure to ease transfers. *Chronicle of Higher Education, 36*(21), A1, A37–38.

Policy Initiatives to Enhance Child Care Staff Compensation

Dan Bellm, Terry Gnezda, Marcy Whitebook, and Gretchen Stahr Breunig

The crises of staffing and quality in child care have deepened, ironically, at the same time that quality child care is hailed for helping parents to enter and stay in the work force, combating welfare dependency and poverty, and promoting children's readiness for school.

Despite the rhetoric, child care programs continue to be funded on a shoestring—and at the expense of child care practitioners, who often mask the true cost of care by working for low wages and few benefits. A national profile of child care settings (Kisker, Hofferth, Phillips, & Farquhar, 1991) confirmed that when adjusted for inflation, real earnings by child care teachers and family child care providers declined by nearly one-quarter since the mid-1970s. Salaries for teachers and providers hover at approximately $10,000 per year.

As documented in the National Child Care Staffing Study (Whitebook, Howes, & Phillips, 1989), the result is high teacher turnover and a decline in the consistency and quality of care that young children receive. An update of the study (Whitebook, Phillips, & Howes, 1993) reveals that the situation is not improving. Fewer than 20% of centers offer full health benefits to all staff. Only 30% of the teachers and assistants interviewed in 1988 are still employed in the same setting. Of the 227 centers in the original study, 34 closed.

Child care programs continue to be funded on a shoestring—and at the expense of child care practitioners, who often mask the true cost of care by working for low wages and few benefits.

Many new developments in related policy arenas promise to affect early childhood education, and the field must play a part in determining their outcome by making its needs heard.

Leadership in the effort to enhance early childhood professional compensation and program quality has shifted between state and federal levels during the past decade. Massachusetts and New York made major strides in upgrading salary levels in the mid- to late 1980s. Advocates increasingly focused their attention on federal child care legislation, resulting in the passage of the Child Care and Development Block Grant (CCDBG) in 1990.

CCDBG implementation has turned much of the focus back to the states, although advocates are working in Washington to remove a variety of restrictive guidelines when the CCDBG is reauthorized. Because of these restrictions, and competing demands for the use of block grant funds, most states have made only modest gains in the areas of compensation and quality improvement. Taken together, however, state initiatives can be seen as building blocks for future, more comprehensive, efforts on behalf of the early childhood profession.

Federal initiatives

The federal government addresses staff compensation in three major areas: military child care, Head Start, and the CCDBG program.

Military child care. Begun as a pilot project to increase teacher salaries at some centers, the Caregiver Personnel Pay Plan launched in 1989 is now an ongoing program within the military child care system that links training to increased compensation. The result has been a dramatic reduction in staff turnover. Major goals are to make early childhood staff salaries competitive with comparable professions within the military, and to break the link between staff compensation and patron fees. Entry-level staff receive increased compensation after completing required training and demonstrating developmentally appropriate practices. The competency-based on-the-job training is modeled after the Child Development Associate (CDA) Credential program. Staff with CDAs, associate, or bachelor's degrees can also increase their compensation by taking advanced training.

Increasing the flexibility of Block grant funds for quality enhancement ranks high on the list of many advocates.

Head Start. The 1990 Head Start Reauthorization included several groundbreaking provisions for staff training and compensation. For the first time, 2% of the Head Start budget was set aside for training; an additional 10% was set aside for quality improvements, including 5% that had to be spent on salaries. After that first year, all Head Start funding increases were required to include a 25% set-aside for quality, with half of this amount dedicated to upgrading salaries. The law mandates that by September 30, 1994, every Head Start classroom have at least one teacher with a Child Development Associate (CDA) credential, a state-awarded certificate that meets or exceeds CDA, or an appropriate early childhood degree. The law also encourages Head Start agencies to adopt salary scales based on training and experience. The 1994 expansion of Head Start maintains these quality provisions.

Child Care and Development Block Grant. Under CCDBG guidelines a state must spend at least 5% of its funds on the improvement of child care quality. Activities include upgrading provider compensation, training, resource and referral services, and licensing. Although the original law allows for additional funds to be spent on quality improvement, federal regulations greatly limit this option. This severely hampers states' abilities to devote funds to staff compensation, with some states forced to shelve their plans to address the compensation issue altogether. Others, however, have managed to use other Block grant funds to study alternative strategies (described later in this chapter), conduct salary surveys, raise reimbursement rates and initiate grant programs. Increasing the flexibility of Block grant funds for quality enhancement ranks high on the list of many advocates for the upcoming re-authorization of the system.

A number of states had undertaken salary enhancement initiatives before passage of the CCDBG, so the Block Grant gave these efforts a major boost. Four basic approaches emerged, some more direct than others. This list is mainly CCDBG related and is not exhaustive; some states and localities have undertaken other initiatives of their own.

Raising reimbursement rates to enhance salaries. Low reimbursement rates are the major way public funding perpetuates low levels of child care compensation. As long as states pay providers to serve low income children less than the going rate for child care services (which is far less than the full cost of care), providers remain torn between serving low-income families and paying themselves decent salaries. For many states, the CCDBG provision that programs can be reimbursed at the market rate has been a significant opportunity to remedy this situation. The major drawback to this strategy, however, is that increased levels of reimbursement can also raise the level of fees paid by parents.

Louisiana documented a significant increase in the market rate, and the state approved a 10% increase in reimbursement rates. Washington put a substantial amount of the new CCDBG funds into rate increases for providers serving subsidized children.

Providers inadvertently tend to depress reimbursement rates by not accurately reporting the true cost of their services. Public and private agencies in Baltimore, Maryland, cosponsored technical assistance workshops for child care providers on calculating true costs, re-establishing rates, setting program budgets, and stabilizing enrollment. New York's 1990 market rate survey led to higher reimbursements, partly due to child care advocates' efforts to help providers develop budgets and charge rates that reflect true costs.

Pennsylvania, a state with particularly depressed reimbursement rates, used much of the direct-service portion of CCDBG funds to raise child care reimbursements that pay parent vouchers. Rates can increase to the 75th percentile of the market rate, as required by the Family Support Act resulting in an increase of 20% in rates in some areas. Connecticut and Washington also used Block Grant funds to revamp their reimbursement sys-

Low reimbursement rates are the major way public funding perpetuates low levels of child care compensation.

State initiatives

tems. For a fuller discussion of rates, see the working paper, "Child Care Reimbursement Rates and their Impact on the Early Childhood Work Force" (National Center for the Early Childhood Work Force, 1994).

Grant programs. Some states developed grants as an alternative way to reward child care programs when there are insufficient funds to increase staff compensation. This approach can also have the advantage of not affecting parent fees.

Wisconsin set aside $600,000 in fiscal year (FY) 91 and an additional $1 million in FY92 for quality improvement grants to help centers and family child care providers meet state standards based on NAEYC accreditation standards but place greater emphases on working conditions, benefits and turnover. Funds may be used for expenses related to becoming accredited and staff training to meet standards. Programs that already meet the standards can use additional funds to directly improve wages and benefits.

Louisiana centers that receive NAEYC accreditation are eligible under the state's CCDBG plan for a 10% reimbursement rate increase. Alaska instituted a program of additional payments per child of low-income families to allow centers and family child care homes to make quality improvements that include salary increases. Oregon is contemplating a similar approach. Washington allocated $1 million for four community pilot projects to explore ways to enhance child care quality and to make recommendations to improve the child care delivery system. Two of these projects, in Seattle and Whatcom County, examined the effect of improved compensation on the quality of child care.

Efforts to link training with better compensation fall into two general categories: reward for professionals who receive advanced training and the expansion of access to training.

Training linked to compensation

Efforts to link training with better compensation fall into two general categories: reward for professionals who receive advanced training (such as mentor programs) and the expansion of access to training (such as scholarships or loan forgiveness programs).

California's Early Childhood Mentor Teacher Program is geared to reward and retain experienced teachers. Using approximately $650,000 of state block grant funds, it establishes a career ladder option for experienced child care teachers by training them to become mentors, thereby earning as much as $3,000 for supervising student teachers in the classroom. The student teachers earn community college credit for a practicum that satisfies state education requirements. The program is intended to reduce teacher turnover and improve the quality and accessibility of the community college training system.

North Carolina's Teacher Education and Compensation Program (TEACH) is designed to assist entry-level staff through scholarships. It uses block grant, state, foundation, and corporate funds. Any full-time teacher or provider is eligible for a scholarship, covering most tuition and book costs, in order to work toward a certificate, diploma, or associate degree in early childhood education. At the end of the scholarship year, center-based teachers agree to continue to work at the sponsoring program for another year in return for a salary increase of at least 5%. TEACH also includes an Early Childhood Model/Mentor Teacher Program.

Tennessee's mentor program started with an annual allocation of $205,000 in block grant funds for three-year pilot projects at two college sites. Ten employees of NAEYC-accredited centers are recruited as mentors at each site and compensated with a stipend. Wisconsin set aside $500,000 of its CCDBG funds for quality improvement projects, including plans for a mentoring program in which skilled teachers are paid to mentor and other teachers are paid to apprentice.

Louisiana allocated CCDBG funds to pay providers to attend workshops and staff development programs. Connecticut allocated state funds for a quality bonus program; teachers and providers who earn a CDA Credential, or accreditation by NAEYC or NAFCC, now receive a direct payment of $5 per child per week for caring for children of state-subsidized families. Texas used some of its $3.3 million fund for teacher scholarships to expand access to affordable training. California and Pennsylvania established Teacher Loan Assumption Programs.

Several states have established planning commissions to develop a model to address staffing and compensation.

Salary surveys, studies, and planning commissions

Several states have established planning commissions to develop a model to address staffing and compensation. Others are convening various groups to study the issues. Most troubling, however, is the finding of the National Center for the Early Childhood Work Force that various states engaged in redesigning their child care training and career development systems are apparently not paying serious attention to the staff compensation issue.

Texas spent $100,000 for a caregiver status survey as the beginning of an effort to examine training and salaries, and to develop a plan linking the two. Connecticut is spending $25,000 of its federal and state funds to develop a state plan for training and staff development that includes an analysis of curricula, a training needs assessment, identification of criteria for prospective programs, and development of salary guidelines. Wisconsin and Oregon also allocated CCDBG funds to establish integrated child care training plans. Wisconsin set aside $75,000 for a career development plan and credentialing project. Washington developed an early childhood training plan to identify the level of training and compensation needed for each child care staff position.

North Carolina set aside $100,000 for a child care worker compensation study to examine new and existing models that promote training and boost child care wages. Oregon spent $20,000 for a commission to research child care salaries and benefits, strategies for improved compensation, and insurance options, but none of the group's recommendations were approved for funding. California allocated funds to study child care worker health benefits and to assess the feasibility of a group health insurance program; meanwhile, such a study was completed in Rhode Island, but the legislature failed to fund any new health care efforts.

Alaska, Pennsylvania, and Wisconsin recently conducted salary sur-

Advocates need to closely monitor the progress of the many states still at the study stages to ensure that the information obtained leads to commitment and action.

veys. The Pennsylvania salary survey was paid for with private funds from local child care associations. New York has two groups researching compensation issues. A state work group is studying the child care work force; the private nonprofit New York State Child Care Coordinating Council is examining career ladder options for child care teachers and family child care providers.

In at least two states, the private sector is also involved in addressing compensation issues. Louisiana officials are working with the Louisiana Public Broadcasting Corporation to make training available statewide to teachers and family child care providers. A group of business leaders in Tennessee has convened to discuss ways to improve child care provider compensation. (Another example of private sector involvement in Hawaii is described by Nina Sazer O'Donnell in this volume.)

Guiding principles for further action

The child care compensation movement has reached an unprecedented stage of breadth and maturity, and has the potential to accomplish major breakthroughs in solving the early childhood work force crisis. In order to maintain momentum, however, four principles are especially critical for the coming years.

Study and build upon current efforts. Which approaches worked best to increase staff compensation? Which fell short? Which make the most effective use of limited funds? In particular, advocates need to closely monitor the progress of the many states still at the study stages to ensure that the information obtained leads to commitment and action. To promote this process and disseminate effective strategies, the National Center for the Early Childhood Work Force Child Care Compensation Initiatives Project began in 1993 with the support of a consortium of foundations including the Carnegie Corporation of New York. This is an ongoing initiative that provides current information through *The Compensation Initiatives Bulletin*, published three times annually.

Break the link between staff salaries and parent fees. Child care consumers cannot be asked to shoulder the tremendous effort it will take to ensure a decent livelihood for all teachers and providers. A serious commitment of public and private funds is essential, and the efforts developed by military child care and Head Start, as well as Wisconsin's Quality Improvement Grants, are particularly good steps in this direction.

Ask the hard questions about early childhood professional development. As states revamp their early childhood career development systems, the efficacy of training programs—and the use of training dollars—must be held to a high standard. Are trainees staying in the field, or are they unable to make a career of it for economic reasons? Are trainees rewarded with professional and economic advancement, or are they forced instead to incur a serious financial burden? What incentives are provided for new and experienced caregivers to obtain training? Are programs limiting the diversity of the work force because only certain individuals can afford to enter such low-paid work?

Professional development programs tend to be evaluated solely on whether training reaches those who need it, and whether participants master the appropriate body of knowledge. But most training programs have yet to confront a mounting hole-in-the-bucket syndrome: each year new teachers must be prepared to replace those who have left the field. Training *must* be linked to efforts to address the compensation crisis, or, sadly, many programs will remain inefficient or even wasteful.

The issues can perhaps be summarized best with a new set of three Rs: *Raise* the floor so that base salaries for newly trained workers entering the field become a livable wage. *Reward* professional development not only with a diploma but with the promise of economic advancement. *Reach* out in order to make ongoing education accessible to everyone in the field.

Broaden the policy focus. Many new developments in related arenas promise to affect early childhood education, and the field must play a part in determining their outcome by making its needs heard. Here are a few examples:

Health care reform: As one of the lowest-paid sectors of the work force, child care staff need a guarantee of universal, quality health coverage, not the lower end of a two-tier system that places comprehensive coverage beyond reach.

Welfare reform: The federal government declared a goal of getting low-income women off welfare after two years. This means the federal government will be looking for jobs, as well as child care, for AFDC recipients. The profession must advocate for a quality child care system, rather than one that places as many children as possible in less-than-quality care. Advocates must also make it clear that child care isn't a viable job unless compensation improves, and that not all mothers will necessarily be suited for or interested in a career working with young children.

Job creation: Federal efforts almost exclude the early childhood profession because the profession can not deliver the kind of high-wage jobs that are most in demand. Advocates need to be able to demonstrate that the field is taking decisive steps to make child care work a more viable option.

National Service Corps: Under such a program, college student loans might be forgiven if graduates commit to a specified period of community service. Child care work, presumably, would qualify—but graduates without early childhood education preparation will need orientation or in-service training, and existing staff should not be supplanted nor left without the resources to train and supervise new staff.

Student loans: Federal efforts such as the Higher Education Act strongly affect the educational options available to students interested in entering

Training must *be linked to efforts to address the compensation crisis, or, sadly, many programs will remain inefficient or even wasteful.*

early childhood education. Financial aid and loan forgiveness programs that target early childhood education students are an essential way to strengthen the work force.

Conclusion

Child care advocates working on states CCDBG plans relate tales of frustration and encouragement. The frustration stems from severe limits on funds, competing claims for these dollars, and in some cases, strong resistance from colleagues and officials to address what has become the most pressing problem for the early childhood profession. Although the cry for improved staff compensation is louder and stronger than ever before, in many states the cry is still not powerful enough to lead to a significant commitment of resources toward a solution.

Advocates are encouraged by the seriousness with which many state policymakers respond to the child care staffing crisis after they become educated through the public hearing and planning processes. In many communities, the primary task is no longer to convince officials and other leaders to address the crisis, but to provide these people with viable solutions. The options described here suggest the wealth of approaches that state and local governments, and other public and private organizations, can pursue.

In many communities, the primary task is no longer to convince officials and other leaders to address the crisis, but to provide these people with viable solutions.

Meanwhile, the Worthy Wage Campaign, coordinated by the National Center for the Early Childhood Workforce, is focusing public attention on child care staffing issues and building support for future allocations of CCDBG funds and other new initiatives. Each time a state CCDBG planning group succeeds in making headway in some area of compensation and training, it becomes easier for other groups to convince their state policymakers to take a step forward. Each experiment is an important building block to help others design increasingly sophisticated and comprehensive models. Despite the obstacles, the prospects have never been brighter to finally make early childhood education a well-recognized and well-rewarded profession.

Bibliography

Bellm, D., & Whitebook, M. (1991). *What states can do to secure a skilled and stable child care work force: Strategies to use the new federal funds for child care quality.* Oakland, CA: Child Care Employee Project.

Kisker, E.E., Hofferth, S.L. Phillips, D.A., & Farquhar, E. (1991). *A profile of child care settings: Early education and care in 1990.* Washington, DC: U.S. Department of Education, Office of the Under Secretary.

Whitebook, M., Howes, C., & Phillips, D.A. (1989). *Who cares? Child care and the quality of care in America.* Final report of the National Child Care Staffing Study. Oakland, CA: Child Care Employee Project.

Whitebook, M., Pemberton, C., Lombardi, J., & Galinsky, E. (1990). *From the floor: Raising child care salaries.* Oakland, CA: Child Care Employee Project.

Whitebook, M., Phillips, D.A., & Howes, C. (1993). *The National Child Care*

Staffing Study revisited: Four years in the life of center-based child care. Oakland, CA: Child Care Employee Project.

Willer, B. (Ed.) (1990). *Reaching the full cost of quality in early childhood programs*. Washington, DC: NAEYC.

Willer, B., Hofferth, S.L., Kisker, E.E., Divine-Hawkins, P., Farquhar, E., & Glantz, F.B. (1991). *The demand and supply of child care in 1990*. Summary findings from *The National Child Care Survey 1990* and *A Profile of Child Care Settings*. Washington, DC: NAEYC.

Resources

The National Center for the Early Childhood Work Force, formerly the Child Care Employee Project, is a policy, advocacy, and research organization dedicated to enhancing the compensation, working conditions and training of child care teachers and family child care providers. The Center also acts as national coordinator of the Worthy Wage Coalition, a grassroots mobilization of caregivers, parents, and others working to confront and reverse the child care staffing crisis. The Coalition sponsors the Worthy Wage Campaign, the focal point of which is a nationwide Worthy Wage Day, held annually during the Week of the Young Child. The National Center also publishes a curriculum, *Working for Quality Child Care*, designed to help students and child care staff become effective advocates for improving quality, salaries, and working conditions in child care programs.

Financing an Optimal Early Childhood Education and Care System: One State's Efforts

Nina Sazer O'Donnell

Three key Hawaii organizations decided to address the challenge of the overwhelming price tag by convening an ECEC Finance Think Tank.

In Hawaii, as in other states, there is an urgent need for a comprehensive system of early childhood education and care that affords families choices among an array of services. Addressing this need became a priority in our state for a variety of reasons, including concerns about school readiness, work force child care, and the general efficacy of preventive social, educational, and health services.

Recognizing these needs, Hawaii embarked on several major early childhood education and care (ECEC) initiatives in recent years. These included efforts to reform public education by the Hawaii Business Roundtable; efforts to address work force child care needs by the Governor's Office of Children and Youth; and other efforts by the state legislature and

The optimal early childhood system will provide all children with equal access to quality education and care resources which are appropriate to families' life circumstances and preferences.

the state Departments of Education (DOE), Health (DOH), and Human Services (DHS). Although rich in prospects, these efforts slowed or stalled because the price tag of a universally accessible ECEC system seemed overwhelming.

In 1991, three key Hawaii organizations decided to address the challenge of the overwhelming price tag by convening an ECEC Finance Think Tank. The Hawaii Community Foundation Robert E. Black Fund, Governor's Office of Children and Youth (OCY), and Hawaii Business Council on Dependent Care brought together seven individuals known for innovative thinking and expertise in finance, development, taxation, economics, and/or public and private financing methods.

Convening a finance think tank

The finance experts were enthusiastic about their assignment and requested a description of an optimal ECEC system and its costs in order to develop feasible ECEC financing strategies. They made two recommendations: (1) expanding the Think Tank to an Advisory Committee representing public and private stakeholders in the current ECEC system (i.e., business, early childhood education professionals, philanthropy, government, higher education, and legislators) and (2) launching an initiative to address these questions. The recommended initiative was launched in May 1992, funded jointly by the Hawaii Community Foundation, Governor's Office of Children and Youth, and the Hawaii Business Roundtable. Sponsors issued Requests for Proposals and selected consultants to carry out the research.

The initiative was designed to culminate in funding strategies to support an optimal statewide ECEC system serving Hawaii's children from birth through age 5 in the year 2000. It was carried out in four steps:

Envisioning an optimal statewide ECEC system

1. Description of the current ECEC system, including supply, demand, costs, funding, and quality;

2. description of an optimal system for the education and care of children from birth through age 5 and their families;

3. cost estimates for an optimal system for Hawaii; and

4. development of funding strategies to pay for the optimal system.

NSO Associates was charged with describing an optimal ECEC system for Hawaii in the year 2000, including options and a recommendation for system management and coordination. Community Resources, Inc. (CRI), a research and planning firm is responsible for describing the current system, determining costs, and developing financing strategies for the optimal system with assistance from NSO Associates.

The vision of the optimal system was developed with inspiration and guidance from a wide range of sources. First, direction came from several recent Hawaii ECEC initiatives created through a process of broad public participation and stakeholder consultation. These included OCY's State Strategic Plan for Workforce Child Care, DOE's plan to serve all 4-year-olds by

The initiative was designed to culminate in funding strategies to support an optimal statewide ECEC system serving Hawaii's children from birth through age 5 in the year 2000.

the year 2000, and recommendations of two education reform reports published by the Hawaii Business Roundtable.

In addition, direction came from throughout the country with the help of national consultants. Dana Friedman and Ellen Galinsky, co-presidents of the Families and Work Institute, were commissioned to conduct a review and analysis of national and international efforts to redesign ECEC systems and to make recommendations for Hawaii's optimal system based on their research. Gwen Morgan, of Work/Family Directions and the Center for Career Development in Early Care and Education served as a consultant to CRI's process of describing the current system and developing costs and financing strategies for the optimal system.

Input from key stakeholders within the state was sought in several ways. A series of interviews were conducted with 35 representatives of key public and private agencies within the state. A discussion draft outlining the vision of an optimal system was distributed to a wide range of individuals and organizations representing various ECEC stakeholders throughout the state. Many of the suggestions made by participants in this process guided the final design of the vision.

The vision of the optimal system is based on the following goal as defined by the Initiative's Advisory Committee:

> "An optimal early childhood education and care system will enable all children to reach their full potential, prepare them for a life of successful learning and enable them to become productive community members. Comprehensive and coordinated services will facilitate appropriate cognitive, physical, and social development in a consistent, healthy, and safe environment by competent and nurturing adults, from birth throughout the early years, in a variety of settings. The optimal early childhood system will provide all children in Hawaii with equal access to quality education and care resources which are appropriate to families' life circumstances and preferences." (Hawaii Governor's Office of Children and Youth, 1994, p. 1)

In the optimal system, quality will be assured in two ways: (1) informed consumers, supported by a state financial aid system, and (2) quality staff, supported by a career development system, adequate compensation, regulations, and monitoring.

The vision includes guiding principles and a description of ECEC services from the perspective of children and families, providers, communities, and employers. It also addresses quality assurance and system planning and coordination. It is intentionally broad and general, because it is based on a commitment to community-based planning and decision making about how the system is operationalized.

The vision includes services to support families as the primary teachers and caregivers of young children as well as support for quality part-time and full-time ECEC programs. It calls for all Hawaii citizens to learn about child growth and development, beginning in elementary school and easy access for families to the health, legal, social, and other services they might need. It also includes a statewide financial aid system to provide families with access to the ECEC programs and services of their choice, regardless of their ability to pay. In the optimal system, quality will be assured in two ways: (1) **informed consumers**, supported by a state financial aid system, and (2) **quality staff**, supported by a career development system, adequate compensation, regulations, and monitoring.

The vision also defines the functions and characteristics of effective planning and coordination. A discussion paper recommending a public/private coordinating mechanism is included as an appendix to the vision statement, although no decisions regarding coordinating mechanisms will be made until communities throughout the state have had the opportunity to discuss and reflect upon the vision and financing strategies and greater consensus is achieved. This strategy acknowledged potentially divisive issues, provided materials for further discussion of the issues, and paved the way for consensus building versus division as the result of premature decision making.

Finally, the vision identifies critical next steps for further system development and capacity building. These steps include creating broad support or buy-in for the vision, recruiting and training additional staff, expanding facilities, promoting quality improvements in existing services, upgrading salaries, continuing development of a career development system, and facilitating community-based planning to operationalize the optimal system.

More than 55 potential new funding mechanisms were identified for the various components of the optimal system.

Developing financing strategies

In addition to identifying the vision, financing strategies to achieve it were also needed. Two finance task forces, made up of a subcommittee of advisory committee members and additional resource people from both the public and private sectors, were established to identify potential financing sources for direct services and capital (buildings and equipment) expenses. More than 55 potential new funding mechanisms were identified for the various components of the optimal system. The mechanisms can be grouped in six broad categories: grants, loans, equity (investments), tax policy, state and local regulations, and reallocation of existing resources. Each of these mechanisms is being analyzed in terms of possible coverage, implementation requirements, feasibility, and local and national precedents for their use. The Advisory Committee is responsible for developing an overall financing strategy that will most likely include a combination of the potential strategies along with existing local, state, federal, and private funding programs.

Table 6 outlines various potential funding mechanisms to support career development as an example of the type of research engaged in by the Finance Task Forces. Although they are not necessarily included in the final recommendations of the Hawaii financing strategy, they have been identified as those that could support career quality assurance activities, including consumer education, career development and incentives to encourage family child care and center-based ECEC. Similar lists were developed to address financing of tuition subsidies, capital improvements, and system planning and coordination.

Some of the mechanisms listed in Table 6 are Hawaii-specific; each

Table 6. Potential Funding Mechanisms that Could Support Career Development

Grants

Hawaii ECEC Fund

State Benefits System for ECEC Providers

Use of Business Marketing Resources to Disseminate ECEC Consumer and Parent Education
   Information

Community-Based Economic Development Grants

Pooled Grant Fund for Business Grantmaking to ECEC

Matching of Employee ECEC Contributions

National Philanthropic Innovative Program Grants

Local Philanthropic Grants

Program-Related Investment Grants

Community Development Block Grants

Loans

Community Redevelopment Agency

ECEC Loan Guarantee Fund

ECEC Revolving Loan Fund

Community Loan Fund

Bank Consortium for ECEC Lending

Program-Related Investment Loans

Micro-Enterprise Peer Lending Organization

Micro-Enterprise Program of Small Businsess Administration

Small Business Administration Loan Guarantee Program

Tax Policy

Income Exclusion for ECEC Providers (allowing a percentage of income to be excluded from
   state taxation)

Tax-exempt Status for Registered Family Child Care Providers

General Tax with Revenues Supporting ECEC

Special Districts for Children within the Counties

Tax Credits to Businesses that Invest in ECEC

State-Level Tax to Support ECEC

State Regulation

Waiver of Current Requirement That Family Child Care Insurance Carriers Have an Office in Hawaii

Reallocation of Resources

Re-allocation of Existing Resources

Note: Financing strategies in the equity (investment) category are omitted here because they do not apply to career development costs.

mechanism, however, could be adapted for other states and could be enhanced by adoption as federal policy. More detailed information about the funding mechanisms—including a description, potential coverage, precedents, implementation requirements, and general evaluation—is included as a technical appendix to the CRI final report, *Financing the Vision*, available from the Hawaii Governor's Office of Children and Youth, P.O. Box 3044, Honolulu, HI 96802.

Although Hawaii's efforts to develop adequate financing for an optimal ECEC system are still in process, we have already identified some factors which have contributed to the project's success. One, already mentioned, was delaying the decision regarding the coordinating mechanism. Another, was the inclusion of business and legislative representatives as well as expert consultants on both early childhood and financing issues. These factors not only helped to achieve high level of ownership for the initiative within the Hawaii business community but also helped to educate advisory committee members whose knowledge in one area (early childhood or finance) typically exceeded knowledge in the other.

One of our most difficult tasks has been understanding language. We have strived hard to avoid early childhood jargon and to take time to ensure that we are using terms consistently and with clarity. One of the greatest challenges has to effectively communicate that quality child care and early childhood education are inseparable.

Another successful strategy was using an outside facilitator, Henry Morgan, a noted business expert from Massachusetts with strong family ties not only to Hawaii but also the early childhood/child care community. Because of his distinguished business career, he is perceived as a peer by the business community. His solid understanding of early childhood education, child care, and community development issues have enabled him to be an effective translator between the business and early childhood/child care communities. His knowledge of and ties to Hawaii added to his credibility. As an "outside expert," he was able to make observations and recommendations that were received differently, and perhaps more effectively, that if they had been made by a local facilitator.

Finally, a critical key to the success of this project has been its collaborative sponsorship. The initiative was jointly funded, planned, and administered by all three project sponsors—government, business, and philanthropy. The joint arrangement has not always been easy, but all involved have recognized its significance as a model for the collaboration that will be required to implement Hawaii's optimal system.

Hawaii Governor's Office of Children and Youth. (1994). *Highlights of Early Childhood Education and Care in Hawaii.* Honolulu, HI: Author.

Lessons learned

One of the greatest challenges has to effectively communicate that quality child care and early childhood education are inseparable.

Reference

Moving Forward toward Financing a Collaborative, Comprehensive Early Childhood Professional Development System

Barbara Ferguson Kamara

Each of these collaborations recognized areas of mutual need and opportunities to maximize existing resources while reducing needless duplication.

The District of Columbia is similar to many states and communities in that more than one public agency is responsible for the professional development of individuals working with children birth through third grade and children up to 15 years of age before and after school. The Office of Early Childhood Development (OECD) in the District of Columbia Department of Human Services Commission on Social Services is responsible for the professional development of the 2,500 personnel in the District's licensed child development centers and family child care homes, and the Early Learning Years branch is responsible for the 3,000 early childhood personnel in the District's public schools. Recognizing the need for collaboration—and the value of working together to maximize available resources—the executive directors of these two agencies established a collaborative working relationship. This chapter outlines some of the concrete examples of this collaboration that helped the District move forward toward a comprehensive early childhood professional development system. It also describes our effort to compile a list of all the current sources of funds for professional development in the Office of Early Childhood Development and the Early Learning Years branch of the D.C. public schools, a critical step toward implementing a comprehensive system of professional development that results in competent personnel and provides them meaningful opportunities for career development.

Specific examples of collaboration

One of the most concrete examples of the ongoing collaboration between the Office of Early Childhood Development and the public schools was the formation of the D.C. Early Childhood Collaborative—a working coalition of businesses, schools, community agencies, human resource development and social service agencies, and other organizations providing services to District children and families—co-chaired by the executive directors of the Office of Early Childhood Development and the Early Learning Years branch of the public schools. The Collaborative's mission is to create a continuum of child development and child care services integrated with family support services, including parent education, literacy training, health, mental health, job training and placement, housing assistance, safety and other essential services.

In addition to the specific efforts of the Early Childhood Collaborative, the collegial relationships between the executive directors of the Office of

Early Childhood Development and the Early Learning Years branch of the D.C. public schools resulted in a number of opportunities for collaboration that maximized the benefits for all concerned. Some examples include the following:

- The Early Learning Years branch included child care directors and teachers in their Early Childhood Teacher Collaborative, offering a variety of professional development experiences including an annual institute.
- The Office of Early Childhood Development transferred funds to the school system to cover the costs of training principals, center directors, family child care providers, and teachers and aides in public schools and community-based programs to successfully integrate children prenatally exposed to drugs in mainstreamed classrooms.
- Public school funds were transferred to Office of Early Childhood Development to provide for grants and training and technical assistance for school-age care, greatly expanding the total funds available.
- The D.C. Public Schools loaned the Office of Early Childhood Development a member of its prekindergarten staff to update a pamphlet that identifies all ongoing early childhood training in the Washington, D.C. metropolitan area.
- The Early Learning Years branch and Office of Early Childhood Development staff worked together to strengthen the early childhood department of our one public university that offers associate, baccalaureate, and master's degrees in early childhood education.
- The D.C. Public Schools loaned one of its social workers to provide training one day a month for individuals who perform the social service function in child development centers.
- The D.C. Early Childhood Collaborative conducted an early childhood training needs assessment across all program types and all professional levels.

Each of these collaborations recognized areas of mutual need and opportunities to maximize existing resources while reducing needless duplication. Fostering these collaborations has enhanced the ability of both the Office of Early Childhood Development and the Early Learning Years branch of the D.C. Public Schools to provide more and better professional development opportunities to early childhood personnel.

In addition to taking advantage of opportunities for collaboration as they arose, we have also pursued a more systematic approach to developing a strategic plan for a collaborative funding and resources strategy to support a comprehensive early childhood professional development system. One of the first tasks in developing a strategic plan was to compile a list of all of the resources currently used within the District to provide early childhood professional development opportunities. We considered funds used for training in specific content areas—infants and toddlers, preschool children, prekindergarten to third grade children, administration, nutrition and food

We have also pursued a more systematic approach to developing a strategic plan for a collaborative funding and resources strategy to support a comprehensive early childhood professional development system.

Compiling a list of available resources

One of the first tasks in developing a strategic plan was to compile a list of all of the resources currently used.

services, special populations such as children with HIV or children with prenatal exposure to substances, substance use, abuse prevention, school-age care, and parenting—as well as funds for training in specific roles—classroom and administrative staff, bus/van drivers and monitors, family child care providers, and social services staff. We included *direct dollars* that are available to the Office of Early Childhood Development or the Early Years Learning branch of the D.C. Public Schools, the *indirect dollars* available to other agencies that can coordinate with or complement our direct dollars, and the *donated services* of individuals and organizations, including corporations, to our in-service and preservice programs.

Although not all of the funding sources that we identified will necessarily be applicable to other states or communities, the compilation should spark ideas for potential funding sources. The compiled list is divided by four major sources: funds from the federal government, funds from agencies within the District government; funds from colleges and universities; and funds from private sources. State funds are not included in this list because the District of Columbia technically does not receive state funds, although it receives allocations from some federal programs as if it were a state.

Federal funds

U.S. Department of Health and Human Services

Child Care and Development Block Grant—The Child Care and Development Block Grant (CCDBG) provides the District, states, and territories federal dollars ($825 million in FY 1992) to expand and enhance child care services. A minimum of five percent of total funds is reserved for quality improvement activities, including training, licensing and monitoring, resource and referral, and salary enhancement. The CCDBG is federally administered by the Administration for Children and Families in the U.S. Department of Health and Human Services. The Office of Early Childhood Development is the lead agency in the District of Columbia, and training is one of the ways that CCDBG quality improvement funds are used.

Child Development Associate Scholarship—This federal program provides a limited amount of money ($1.2 million in FY 92) for states to provide scholarships and training for individuals seeking a Child Development Associate (CDA) Credential. In the District, these funds are administered by the Office of Early Childhood Development.

Dependent Care Planning and Development Grant—Dependent Care Planning and Development Block Grant funds have been available since the mid 1980s to plan, develop, establish, expand and improve school-age child care (60% of funds) and state and local dependent care resource and referral services (40% of funds). In FY 92, $13 million was appropriated for this program. Administered in the District by the Office of Early Childhood Development, funds, as in many states, have used to train school-age child care providers.

Head Start—The federal Head Start program has traditionally been the largest source of early childhood training funds. In addition to the training funds included in each Head Start program's budget, the federal Head Start Bureau funds Resource Access Projects (RAP) on special needs issues as well as Regional Resource Centers in each of the federal regions. Head Start directors are eligible to participate in a competitive selection process to attend management training seminars held each summer at the University of California at Los Angeles, supported by Johnson & Johnson. Federal guidance now encourages greater collaboration between Head Start and other community-based child care and early education programs, including for training. The Office of Early Childhood Development is the District government liaison with the D.C. Head Start program.

Center for Disease Control and Prevention (CDCP)—The Office of Early Childhood Development is collaborating with a Howard University project on violence treatment and prevention funded by CDCP. The two-pronged approach sends teams into centers that have been directly affected by violence to work with the staff, children, and parents and provides violence prevention training and technical assistance to staff, parents, and children in other centers in the area. The project also works with school-age children and their teachers at a two nearby elementary schools.

Center for Substance Abuse Prevention—Funds are used to sponsor seminars and purchase materials related to substance abuse prevention for early childhood practitioners.

U.S. Department of Education

Chapter II program, Elementary and Secondary Education Act—The Elementary and Secondary Education Act (ESEA) is the largest source of federal support for public education. Chapter II funds are administered at local discretion and professional development is one of the purposes for which funds may be spent. A portion of the District's funds are being used to train teachers on working with parents and the community.

Part H and Part B of the Individuals with Disabilities Education Act (IDEA)—The Individuals with Disabilities Education Act (IDEA), formerly known as the Education of the Handicapped Act, provides four main sources of funding of potential use for early childhood professional development. Two sources are grants to states—the Program for Infants and Toddlers with Disabilities (referred to as Part H) and the Preschool Grants Program for 3 to 5 year olds (referred to as Section 619 of Part B). The other two sources are federal demonstration projects—the Early Education Program for Children with Disabilities (EEPCD) and Special Education Personnel Development and Parent Training Projects. With growing recognition of the importance of inclusion—and the legal requirements established by the Americans with Disabilities Act—increasing numbers of children with disabilities

With growing recognition of the importance of inclusion, increasing numbers of children with disabilities and other special learning needs are being cared for in community-based programs.

and other special learning needs are being cared for in community-based early childhood and child care programs. In the District, both the Office of Early Childhood Development and the Early Learning Years branch of the public schools access available funds that can be used to provide training to early childhood personnel to work with children with special needs.

Funds from Part H provide training on infant and toddler development for child development staff and family child care providers. The Section 619 of Part B funds support training for public school and non-public school personnel on effective integration and mainstreaming of children, work with parents, and intervention strategies for children with developmental delays or at risk of delay, including children prenatally exposed to substances. The District used some of its Comprehensive System of Personnel

Federal guidance now encourages greater collaboration between Head Start and other community-based child care and early education programs, including for training.

Development funds under IDEA to pay for public school educational aides to obtain their baccalaureate degree in special education. The executive directors of the Office of Early Childhood Development and the Early Learning Years are members of the Comprehensive System of Personnel Development Advisory Committee.

Library Services and Construction Act—This federal program is designed to promote greater community access to libraries and their services. Funds under this program are being used by the Public Library system in collaboration with the Office of Early Childhood Development to send a librarian with a library van to visit licensed family child care homes once a month.

U.S. Department of Agriculture

Child and Adult Care Food Program—The Child and Adult Care Food Program is administered by the U.S. Department of Agriculture (USDA) to provide federal funds and USDA-donated food to nonresidential child care and adult day care facilities so that they can serve nutritious meals and snacks to program participants. Although all family child care providers and nonprofit centers are eligible to participate, for-profit centers must serve a certain percentage of income-eligible families in order to participate. States participating in the program must provide training to recipients, although the amount and type of training varies across the states according to state regulations.

Nutrition Education Training (NET) Program—This federal program provides nutritional training for personnel in programs eligible to participate in Child Nutrition programs and for dissemination of nutrition information to children enrolled in these programs. The Office of Early Childhood Development, in collaboration with the Mayor's Advisory Committee on Food, Nutrition, and Health and the Family Life Science Department of the University of the District of Columbia, used NET funds to provide a 15-clock hour course for center staff for which they received one regular college credit upon fulfilling the course requirements and paying the appropriate course fee.

Cooperative Extension Service—The cooperative extension system provides a unique partnership among the federal government, state land-grant universities, and local government (county, parish, or city). Extension home economists originally worked mainly with rural-based extension homemakers; today, extension services are available in nearly all of the nation's 3,150 counties, offering training and information on a variety of issues, including child care and child development. Training for personnel in centers and homes focuses on parent education and involvement.

U.S. Department of Justice

Weed & Seed Program—A comprehensive, multi-agency approach to combatting violent crime, drug use, and gang activity in high-crime neighbor-hoods, the Weed and Seed program provides funds that the D.C. Office of Early Childhood Development used to provide school-age care.

National Aeronautics and Space Administration (NASA)

Aerospace Education Services program—NASA assigned a full-time staff person to design and implement math and science training for teachers in conjunction with the District of Columbia Early Childhood Collaborative under this program.

Funds from agencies within the District of Columbia government

In compiling the list of available funding resources, we considered all of the services provided by other agencies within the District government. In many cases, these services represented indirect dollars that could coordi-nate with or complement direct funds.

Public Library—The library offers workshops for child care providers, in-cluding a monthly series for instructional materials preparation, and of-fers weekly sessions for preschool children featuring films and stories.

Office of Business and Economic Development—This office offers techni-cal assistance to programs on how to finance centers.

Department of Recreation and Parks—A number of preschool and school-age training and drug-prevention activities are provided through this de-partment.

Commission of Public Health, Office of Maternal and Child Health Pedi-atrics AIDS Project—This project offers weekly and Saturday sessions on caring for children with HIV.

Commission of Public Health, Agency for AIDS Activities—On-site training for working with children infected with HIV is provided in infant centers.

Department of Employment Services (DOES)—The SMART (Single Moth-ers are Resources Too) program is a collaborative effort between the D. C. Public Schools and DOES among other groups to provide employment train-ing, education, and support services to AFDC and low-income persons in-terested in becoming educational aides, child care assistants, teachers, in-fant caregivers, and family child care providers. Participants can receive up to 9 college credits for training based upon the CDA requirements.

Department of Consumer and Regulatory Affairs, Nutrition—The child care licensing unit of this department has a nutritionist who provides train-ing for small groups of center staff on nutrition education strategies.

District-Appropriated Child Care Subsidy Program—This program supple-ments federal funds for nutrition training for family child care providers.

Office of Early Childhood Development—This office is the lead agency for the Child Care and Development Block Grant, the Dependent Care Plan-

Office of Early Childhood Development sponsors a Child Care Calendar Line—a telephone recording available 24 hours a day that provides regularly updated information on training sessions and conferences.

ning and Development Block Grant, the Child Development Associate Scholarship Program, Boarder Babies project, and Children and Substance Abuse Project. It also sponsors a Child Care Calendar Line, a telephone recording available 24 hours a day that provides regularly updated information on training sessions and conferences.

District of Columbia Public School System—The public school system is implementing the following programs:

- *Parents As Teachers Program*—provides training for infant and toddler program staff and home visitors
- *Child Care Courses*—Classes for high school students and adults are offered during the day and in the evening
- *Teaching Profession Program*—This program enrolls 84 students annually starting with ninth graders; 100% of the graduates have enrolled in college.
- *Early Childhood Teacher Collaborative*—This program sponsors an annual institute open to the entire early childhood community along with monthly support groups and workshops.
- *Responsive Environment*—These in-service courses stress such topics as whole language and child development.
- *Center for Education Change*—The Center sponsored an early childhood training summit in April 1993.

Funds available through colleges and universities

The District of Columbia is home to a number of public and private institutions of higher learning. Following are some of the programs and sources of early childhood professional development funds provided by colleges and universities.

University of the District of Columbia (UDC)—The UDC offers a number of professional development opportunities. *The Center for Applied Research and Urban Policy* conducted a research project in collaboration with Office of Early Childhood Development focusing on boarder babies, children of substance abusers, and children in environments in which there is substance abuse. A conference and training session for a wide range of personnel resulted from this research. *The College of Education and Human Ecology* implements a scholarship program with Office of Early Childhood Development that enables child care center personnel and family child care providers to take designated courses for which they receive undergraduate or graduate credit. *The Department of Social Work and Social Welfare* offers coursework and technical assistance for individuals performing the social services function in child care and Head Start programs. Finally, *cooperative extension services* are operated out of UDC.

Howard University—The *Small Business Development Center* provides technical assistance to family child care providers and operators of centers. *The Howard University Child Development Center* offers training in AIDS awareness and caring for children with HIV. *The Howard University Violence Preven-*

Howard University has a mobile team to provide consultation to staff, parents, and children in child care centers located in areas impacted by community violence.

tion Program sponsors workshops for school-age children and staff and has a mobile team to provide consultation to staff, parents, and children in child care centers located in areas impacted by community violence.

George Washington University—A U.S. Department of Education grant is being used to train child care staff to integrate students with disabilities and other special learning needs.

Georgetown University Affiliated Program—In collaboration with the D.C. Department of Human Services Child Day Care Services Division's Advisory Committee, a training curriculum for child development personnel working with special populations was piloted and field tested.

Private sources

Often overlooked in the compilation of existing resources are the funds provided by private resources. Private resources, however, add to the overall amount of funds available for the provision of professional development opportunities. Some examples of these resources include the following.

- Vendors of early childhood materials and equipment had their consultants conduct training for District early childhood personnel or provided funds to enable an Office of Early Childhood Development-selected consultant to conduct training.
- The Women in Business Committee of the District of Columbia Chamber of Commerce co-sponsored an administrative course for center directors.
- The Council of Governments, a regional group of governments in the metropolitan Washington, D.C. area, sponsored workshops and seminars on such topics as fire safety with young children, multicultural integration in early childhood programs, options for serving children with special needs, and using space in public housing for child care facilities.
- The Smithsonian Museum sponsored seminar on multiculturalism for early childhood program staff.
- Four hospitals in the District of Columbia offer training for early childhood and child care providers on health topics, including general training on health and safety issues, seminars on children prenatally exposed to drugs and support groups for their parents and grandparents, and caring for children with HIV. The local SAFE KIDS Coalition, supported by a children's hospital, sponsored seminars, materials, and information fairs on various aspects of child safety.
- The local chapter of the National Association of Social Workers, Social Work Emeritus Project conducted an assessment of needs of persons who perform the social services function in early childhood programs followed by an orientation training. Working with the Department of Social Work and Social Welfare at the University of the District of Columbia, the group explored the possibility of establishing a credit-bearing course based on materials developed by Head Start.

- The American Business Collaborative, a national group of corporations who pooled their resources to support quality dependent care initiatives, provided funding to a local resource and referral agency to conduct training for child care providers.
- Local consultant organizations or individual professionals donated their services to support training efforts.
- Community foundations provided funds to various groups, generally, non-profit organizations, to conduct specific training sessions.
- Early childhood professional and provider associations conducted training for their members and for non-members who pay a fee.
- Centers and other programs provided inservice training using funds from their program budgets.
- Early childhood professionals added to the total funds available for professional development when they pay for professional development opportunities.

Compiling this broad list of direct, indirect, and donated dollars available for professional development within the District of Columbia has enabled the Early Childhood Collaborative to further our strategic planning efforts. Together we can and together we will MOVE FORWARD a comprehensive system of early childhood professional development in the District of Columbia.

Often overlooked private resources add to the overall amount of funds available for the provision of professional development opportunities.

Resources

Davison, J.L. (1993). *Moving forward: A collaborative approach to early childhood professional development in the District of Columbia*. Washington, DC: Office of Early Childhood Development and D.C. Public Schools Early Learning Years Branch.

D.C. Government. (1992). *Child day care and development programs in the District of Columbia*. Washington, DC: Office of Early Childhood Development.

D.C. Government & University of the District of Columbia. (1990). *Boarder babies and drug affected children in the District of Columbia: A case for public/private partnerships comprehensive planning and coordinated services*.

Hargett-Lawton, C. (1993). *Our children's future: A collaborative approach to early childhood professional development in the District: A survey of training needs*. Washington, DC: The D.C. Early Childhood Collaborative.

Lombardi, J. (1992). *Know your state's financing resources: A guide to funding Career Development in Early Care and Education*. Boston: The Center for Career Development in Early Care and Education.

Morgan, G., S. Azer, J. Costley, A. Genser, I.F. Goodman, J. Lombardi, & B. McGimsey. (1993). *Making a career of it: The state of the states report on career development in early care and education*. Boston: The Center for Career Development in Early Care and Education.

Sugarman, J.M. (1991). *Building early childhood systems: A resource handbook*. New York: Child Welfare League of America.

List of Contributors

Sheri L. Azer
Research Associate
The Center for Career
    Development in Early Care and
    Education
Boston, MA

Dan Bellm
Writer, Editor
National Center for the Early
    Childhood Work Force
Washington, DC

Paula Jorde Bloom
Professor
National-Louis University
Evanston, IL

Sue Bredekamp
Director of Professional
    Development
National Association for the
    Education of Young Children
Washington, DC

Gretchen Stahr Breunig
National Center for the Early
    Childhood Work Force
Washington, DC

Nancy Cohen
Research Associate
Yale University Bush Center
New Haven, CT

Joan Costley
Associate Director
The Center for Career
    Development in Early Care and
    Education
Boston, MA

Kimberly Elliott
Editorial/Administrative Associate

The Center for Career
    Development in Early Care and
    Education
Boston, MA

Ann J. Francis
Director, Virginia Tech Resource
    and Referral Service
Virginia Polytechnic Institute and
    State University
Blacksburg, VA

Brenda Fyfe
Associate Professor and
Chairperson, Department of
    Education, and Director of
    Experiential and Individualized
    Learning
Webster University
St. Louis, MO

Andrea Genser
Executive Director
The Center for Career
    Development in Early Care and
    Education
Boston, MA

Terry Gnezda
Consultant
National Center for the Early
    Childhood Work Force
Washington, DC

Irene F. Goodman
Executive Director
Sierra Research Associates
Boston, MA

Edward Greene
Director of Programs
Center for Educational Programs
New York, NY

Kay Hollestelle
Executive Director
Children's Foundation
Washington, DC

Betty L. Hutchison
Associate Professor
National-Louis University
Evanston, IL

Julienne Johnson
Senior Program Associate
Child Care and Development
    Division
Children's Defense Fund
Washington, DC

Elizabeth Jones
Faculty, Human Development
Pacific Oaks College
Pasadena, CA

Barbara Ferguson Kamara
Executive Director
Department of Human Services,
    Commission on Social Services
Office of Early Childhood
    Development
Washington, DC

Cecelia Alvarado Kuster
Professor/Department Chair
Early Childhood Education
Santa Barbara City College
Santa Barbara, CA

J. Ronald Lally
Director, Center for Child and
    Family Studies
Far West Laboratory
Sausalito, CA

Peter Mangione
Senior Research Associate
Center for Child and Family
    Studies
Far West Laboratory
Sausalito, CA

Jan McCarthy
Director, Center for Child &
    Family Studies
College of Education
University of South Florida
Tampa, FL

List of Contributors cont.

Janet B. McCracken
Early Childhood Education
    Consultant
Subjects & Predicates
Gettysburg, PA

Bettina McGimsey
Project Manager/Research
The Center for Career
    Development in Early Care and
    Education
Boston, MA

Kathy Modigliani
Director of the Family Child Care
    Project
Wheelock College
Boston, MA

Gwen Morgan
Founding Director
Wheelock College Center for
    Career Development in Early
    Care and Education
Boston, MA

Kenneth E. Nye
Research Associate/
Executive Administrative Assistant
State Board of Education
Nashville, TN

Nina Sazer O'Donnell
President
NSO Associates
Kailua, HI

Susan O'Connor
Research Associate
The School-Age Child Care Project
    Center for Research on Women
Wellesley College
Wellesley, MA

Carol Brunson Phillips
Executive Director
The Council for Early Childhood
    Professional Recognition
Washington, DC

Barbara J. Smith
Executive Director
Division for Early Childhood of
    the Council for Exceptional
    Children
Pittsburgh, PA

Bernard Spodek
Professor
Early Childhood Education
University of Illinois
Champaign, IL

Andrew J. Stremmel
Assistant Professor
Family and Child Development
Virginia Polytechnic Institute and
    State University
Blacksburg, VA

Karen VanderVen
Professor
School of Social Work
University of Pittsburgh
Pittsburgh, PA

David P. Weikart
President
High/Scope Educational Research
    Foundation
Ypsilanti, MI

Marcy Whitebook
Founding Executive Director 1977–
    1994
Currently Senior Research Policy
    Advisor
National Center for the Early
    Childhood Work Force, formerly
    the Child Care Employee
    Project
Oakland, CA

Cheryl-Ann Whitehead
President
Windflower
Colorado Springs, CO

Barbara Willer
Director of Public Affairs
National Association for the
    Education of Young Children
Washington, DC

Barbara L. Wolfe
Early Childhood Project
    Coordinator
University of Wisconsin-Eau Claire
Eau Claire, WI

Carol Lou Young-Holt
Consultant
Far West Laboratory
Sausalito, CA

Information about NAEYC

NAEYC is . . .

a membership-supported organization of people committed to fostering the growth and development of children from birth through age 8. Membership is open to all who share a desire to serve and act on behalf of the needs and rights of young children.

NAEYC provides . . .

educational services and resources to adults who work with and for children, including

- *Young Children, the* journal for early childhood educators
- **Books, posters, brochures,** and **videos** to expand your knowledge and commitment to young children, with topics including infants, curriculum, research, discipline, teacher education, and parent involvement
- An **Annual Conference** that brings people from all over the country to share their expertise and advocate on behalf of children and families
- **Week of the Young Child** celebrations sponsored by NAEYC Affiliate Groups across the nation to call public attention to the needs and rights of children and families
- **Insurance plans** for individuals and programs
- **Public affairs** information for knowledgeable advocacy efforts at all levels of government and through the media
- The **National Academy of Early Childhood Programs,** a voluntary accreditation system for high-quality programs for children
- The **National Institute for Early Childhood Professional Development,** providing resources and services to improve professional preparation and development of early childhood educators
- The **Information Service,** a centralized source of information sharing, distribution, and collaboration

For free information about membership, publications, or other NAEYC services . . .

call NAEYC at 202-232-8777 or 800-424-2460, or write to NAEYC, 1509 16th Street, N.W., Washington, DC 20036-1426.

FACING
HISTORY
AND
OURSELVES

**A FACING HISTORY
AND OURSELVES
STUDY GUIDE**

Facing History and Ourselves is an international educational and professional development organization whose mission is to engage students of diverse backgrounds in an examination of racism, prejudice, and antisemitism in order to promote the development of a more humane and informed citizenry. By studying the historical development of the Holocaust and other examples of genocide, students make the essential connection between history and the moral choices they confront in their own lives. For more information about Facing History and Ourselves, please visit our website at www.facinghistory.org.

Cover art credits: *Rural home image*, General Research & Reference Division, Schomburg Center for Research in Black Culture, The New York Public Library, Astor, Lenox and Tilden Foundations. *Young girl image*, Martin Barraud, Getty Images. Both images reproduced with permission.

ISBN-13: 978-1-940457-07-9

ISBN-10: 1-940457-07-6